CONTENTS

INTRODUCTION

Halloween is the one time of the year when we can be whoever we want to be. We can dress how we want to dress, throw whatever kind of party we want to throw, and actually be rewarded for our wildest ideas. In fact, it's the year's most creative holiday, so why not push the envelope and try out some crazy, memorable stunts? Let's make the kids actually earn their candy. Let's dress up in fabulously stupid costumes. Let's make all of our guests laugh (and maybe shriek) when they fall for our pranks. Let's create some outrageously large yard art and perfectly disgusting party food and drinks. Let's have some good ole creepy Halloween fun.

Extreme Halloween will help you make this Halloween the coolest one ever. Here's how:

1 **YOU WILL HAVE THE CREEPIEST HOUSE ON YOUR BLOCK, POSSIBLY IN YOUR ENTIRE TOWN!** This book contains projects and pranks for your front yard (including a few magic tricks) that might seem likely to get you thrown in jail, but instead will make you and your house wildly popular with your friends and neighbors. You will stun, frighten, and freak out everyone who stops by.

2 **YOU WILL THROW THE SILLIEST, WILDEST, WEIRDEST HALLOWEEN PARTY EVER.** You have never seen food, drinks, and activities in such questionable taste. (Some say they border on revolting, but you'll be the judge of that.) You will second-guess yourself the entire time you are preparing for the party—and your confidantes will just shake their heads when you tell them your plans. But in the end, your party will be awesome and one of a kind. People will talk about it for months (you may become a local Halloween legend), and everyone will be wondering what kind of crazy things you have in store for them next year.

To create this book, I started with a thousand ideas, many of them truly tasteless. From that list, we picked the best of the best (or is that the worst of the worst?) and published them here. What were our criteria, you ask? The ideas had to be surprising and fun—and so gross and disgusting they were sure to offend someone. After all, if everyone likes something it can't be cool. So if you want a book that contains cute Halloween crafts that everyone will just adore, I suggest you shop at the supermarket.

But if you want recipes and projects that will thrill your friends and favorite neighbors (and horrify everyone else), read on.

Think of Halloween as a battleground between the cool people (us) and the goody-goodies (them). We've won trick-or-treating, booze, pumpkins, and haunted houses, but they still control a number of key Halloween traditions. In the future we'll take over more aspects of our favorite holiday, but I predict that the goody-goodies will never surrender their domination of certain categories. The goody-goodies will always have the best placemats and doilies, and they will likely never admit defeat when it comes to making cupcakes. But we're going to sneak attack them by taking over the quaint arts of Halloween centerpieces, invitations, and decorations.

My ultimate goal is to inspire you to take action. Let's turn Halloween upside down. Let's trick out our yards with ferocious monsters and hilarious pranks. Let's dress in completely moronic costumes and throw totally outrageous Halloween parties. Together we can rewrite Halloween traditions. It will be our holiday from now on. And it will be badass.

Super-Cool Tools and Materials

IN MY TOWN, the home center and the craft store are separated only by a parking lot. I asked my wife if I could buy an RV and move in between the two of them. She said I would still have to come home once a week to take out the trash, so I just drive there a couple of times a week instead. These are the items I have found there that make me truly happy. You will find that these awesome tools and materials are used again and again to create the projects and recipes in this book.

- **ANGLE GRINDER:** Most people use angle grinders to strip rust off cars, but I use mine to take the outer layer off all sorts of things. I strip the skin off pumpkins, the bark off logs, and the paint off any old thing. It works fast and leaves a big mess.

- **CORDLESS TOOLS:** I used to speak out against cordless tools. "Back in my day, drills plugged into walls," I would say. That was before I cut an extension cord with an electric hedge trimmer for the third time. Going cordless is a great idea if you are klutzy. I'm klutzy.

- **DECK SCREWS:** Nails are totally overrated. They are hard to remove and you can't reuse them. Deck screws turn any project into a giant Lego set that you can take apart and put back together again. Three cheers for deck screws!

- **DRILL:** Since I drill stuff instead of hammering it, I always have a drill handy. My editor would like me to mention that it is an electric drill because some Amish guy in Pennsylvania still uses a hand drill, and to accommodate him, I must mention that I opt for an electric drill.

- **DRYWALL SAW:** These things absolutely kill a pumpkin. They are cheap and easy to use.

- **DUCT TAPE:** Sometimes, when my glue gun is not handy, I use duct tape. Tape is as good as glue except it's only sticky on one side. Duct tape is like half glue.

- **FOOD:** I like to play with food. From reading this book, you would probably guess that pudding, whipped cream, bananas, and barbecue ribs are my favorites and you would be absolutely correct.

- **FOOD COLORING:** Want to make food look disgusting but still taste good? Me, too! The secret is food coloring. I buy most of my food coloring at the supermarket, but if you need a strange color, like fluorescent green or black, go to the craft store.

- **GLUE GUN:** When you want to attach a widget to a whoosit, a glue gun is a magical thing.

- **JIGSAW:** Long ago I stopped cutting things by hand and put my jigsaw to work. Sure, it works well for woodworking, but if you don't mind eating a splinter or two, you can use it on meat as well. Mostly though, I recommend jigsaws for attacking unsuspecting pumpkins.

- **REBAR:** Construction workers use rebar to add strength to floors, driveways, and concrete structures. It is a tough, rough, rusty steel reinforcement bar that home centers carry but mortals rarely touch. I like to use it mainly because most people don't. I push the home center envelope that way. I'll use anything they're selling.

- **ROPE, PULLEYS, CLEATS, AND HOOKS:** Home centers have an amazing amount of ropey stuff, much of which is useful for creating creepy illusions that involve hanging things.

- **TRASH:** My favorite material to work with is trash. A walk on trash night almost always yields something to work with. I like trash best of all because if I make a mistake, the net result is that I moved something from a neighbor's trash into my trash. No harm done!

- **2x4s:** How can these be so cheap? You can buy a giant piece of wood for less than the price of a single pen. That is really weird. That's why I like to build stuff with 2x4s. The remnants and mistakes make great campfire wood.

- **WILTON BAKE EASY! SPRAY:** This stuff is available at craft stores or baking supply stores. Spray it on and nothing you bake will stick to the pan. Nothing sticks. Nothing. Not once. Never. No chance.

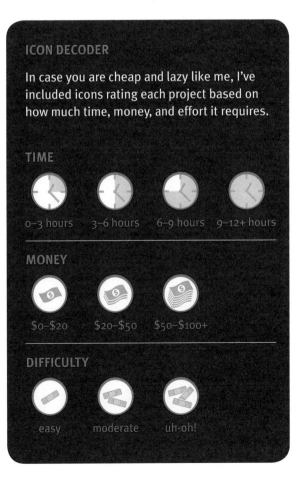

ICON DECODER

In case you are cheap and lazy like me, I've included icons rating each project based on how much time, money, and effort it requires.

TIME

| 0–3 hours | 3–6 hours | 6–9 hours | 9–12+ hours |

MONEY

| $0–$20 | $20–$50 | $50–$100+ |

DIFFICULTY

| easy | moderate | uh-oh! |

EXTREME YARD TRICKS

CREATE THE CREEPIEST HOUSE ON THE BLOCK

Extreme Halloween is divided into two sections because there are two types of people who come to your house on Halloween: Those people who you will let inside and those who have no chance. We are going to play tricks on both groups, certainly, but this section focuses on freaking out kids and other neighbors you don't really know. I call it "Extreme Yard Tricks" because you will stage these tricks in your front yard or on your front porch or walkway. Some of the pranks are stationary, such as the Baby-Eating Yard Monster, while others like the Zip-Line Ghost move around for maximum impact. Some pranks, such as a Coffin Full of Scares, are for Halloween night only, while others can be laughed at for more than a month. Whichever tricks or pranks you choose, people will remember your house next year. I just hope those people aren't the authorities.

yard sculptures that include 16 pumpkins and 62 carrots. I mean, who carves a hundred bucks' worth of perfectly good produce then leaves it in their yard to rot? Yet I've become extremely popular with the neighborhood kids—and the local rabbit population, too. While you can certainly think of better ways to spend your money, like a gas-powered bar stool or an air-conditioned toilet seat, the amazing thing about the Creepy Millipede is that it takes less than two hours to build.

YOU'LL NEED:

- **CARVING TOOLS: jigsaw** (or pumpkin-carving saw), **drill with ½-inch bit** (electric or manual), and **mallet, hammer, or big rock** (in a pinch)

- **16 (or more) pumpkins for body segments** (they should gradually increase in size, if possible)

- **62 carrots** (or 4 carrots per pumpkin)

- **One 6-foot-long piece of rebar** (steel reinforcement bar found at your local home center)

16 Segments Make 1 Worm

1. Select one pumpkin for the millipede's head, then using the jigsaw and drill, **CARVE THE FACE**. I can offer very little advice here, as I have never actually seen a millipede in real life, and in the few photos I have seen, they appear to have almost no head.

2. What I do know for a fact is that millipedes have two antennae, so **DRILL TWO HOLES** in the top of the head and **INSERT TWO CARROTS**, then set the head aside.

3. **LINE UP** the remaining 15 or more pumpkins from smallest (representing the tip of the tail) to biggest (let's call it the neck, though I have no idea if millipedes actually have necks), where you will ultimately attach the head.

4 **DRILL FOUR HOLES** in each body segment, two on each side of each pumpkin. You will insert carrot legs in the holes later, so before you drill all the holes, check one to be sure the stem end of a carrot fits snugly in it. (Having trouble? Here's a tip: Remove any carrot greens first.)

Assemble Your Creeper

5 **BEND THE REBAR** into a big arc. You will need to secure the bar under something to bend it (I used the two legs of my workbench), then **PULL, DON'T PUSH** on the bar. Wear gloves so you don't get slashed. It's not a difficult job, but you'll feel like Hercules anyway. (I won't tell if you pound your chest and hoot a few times afterward; after all, you just bent metal with muscle!)

6 **POUND** one end of the bent rebar into the ground. You'll need to drive it far enough in to hold up the weight of the neck (have we decided if millipedes have necks yet?), about 2 feet deep should be adequate.

7 **CHOP OFF** the stems, then **DRILL** holes all the way through four of the biggest pumpkins. **THREAD** these pumpkins onto the rebar to create the thing we are calling the millipede's neck. Drill a hole in the bottom of the millipede's head, but don't drill all the way through the pumpkin, only halfway. Thread it onto the rebar to top off the neck.

62 Legs and Counting

8 **ARRANGE** the remaining pumpkins in a winding chain behind the neck. **INSERT** four carrot legs (stem end first) into the holes you carved on the sides of each pumpkin. Pretty soon, your sculpture will begin to look like a crazed millipede, only giant-size—mine was 15 feet long!

Creep Everyone
Out with This
Creepy Crawler

More Backyard Beasts You Can Build

I've included instructions for constructing a giant millipede, scorpion, and sea serpent (along with a mythical creature I like to call the Baby-Eating Yard Monster). But feel free to invent your own outrageous backyard behemoths. Here are some wicked ideas to get you started. (TIP: Reptiles, living or extinct, seem to be a category worth exploring.)

- GIANT SEA TURTLE: These are endangered creatures, so you can feel virtuous about raising awareness about their plight when really you just want to carve something cool. You'll need a huge pumpkin to create the shell—and a Dremel rotary tool (or square-tipped chisel) to carve the diamond pattern on the top.

- DRAGON: I know, I already carved a backyard sea monster. But your dragon could have wings or breathe fire (though my publisher insists that you do so at your own risk).

- DINOSAUR: This would be similar to the sea monster or dragon. For details, ask a ten-year-old; they tend to possess encyclopedic knowledge about the distinguishing characteristics of different dinosaurs.

- ALLIGATOR: Those Hubbard squashes already look just like an alligator's head. Why not carve an evil face, then add a few gourds and squashes to create a body, tail, and legs?

- ARMADILLO: The plated exoskeleton of this critter could be admirably re-created using a pumpkin shell.

- RATTLESNAKE: Pie pumpkins would work well for the body. Consider a squash head and a carrot for the rattle on the tip of the tail.

- BULLFROG: Some large pumpkins get fairly ungainly. In fact, some look a lot like a squatting frog. You could complete the transformation.

- CERBERUS: A three-headed dog that guards the gates of Hell—that is my kind of pumpkin carving. I suggest butternut squashes for the three heads. For the rest, you are on your own!

entire neighborhood prepared, which is why I built this simple yard display. You should make one for your yard, too. Your neighbors will thank you when the zombies rise from the dead.

YOU'LL NEED:

- **1 pumpkin** (larger than a human head)
- **CARVING TOOLS: jigsaw** (or pumpkin-carving saw), **big metal spoon**
- **Old gloves, shirt, and pants** (even the undead wear clothes)
- **2 old shoes** (or one old shoe and a fake foot from a Halloween supply store)
- **Plenty of dirt** (3 cubic feet if you plan to buy some)
- **Shovel and spade** (for digging the grave)

Kill It

1 In order for your pumpkin to **RISE** from the dead, you have to kill it first. So **SCALP** it, **GUT** it, and **CARVE** a pained expression. Your jigsaw and big metal spoon are the only **MURDER WEAPONS** you'll need.

Bury It

2 **SELECT** a spot in your lawn that is **VISIBLE** to passersby. We happened to have a low spot in our yard that benefited from a little more dirt.

3 Carefully **ARRANGE** the old pants, gloves, and shoes. Remember this isn't a scarecrow. Pose the clothes so they look like a zombie is trying to **BREAK FREE** from beneath the earth's surface. **ADD** the anguished pumpkin head.

Disturb the Gravesite

4 Use $1/3$ of the dirt to **DEFINE** the boundaries of the gravesite. My experience of **GRAVE DIGGING** and zombies is limited, but I **SPREAD OUT** a layer of dirt approximately 8 feet long by 3 feet wide, and it seemed to do the job.

5 **POUR** $1/3$ of the dirt over the pumpkin's head and clothes. The zombie should be almost **COMPLETELY COVERED** now.

6 We all know that zombies try to **CLAW** their way out of their graves. Adjust your zombie's clothes to make it look like he is trying to **RISE FROM THE DEAD**. Pull one of the knees of the pants out of the dirt. **POSITION** one of the shoes (or the bare foot) so it looks like it is pushing out of the ground. Do the same with one of the gloves. **SHAKE** some dirt on top of the pumpkin head and inside its cavities. If this pumpkin had been **BURIED ALIVE**, it would certainly have some dirt in its mouth.

7 Graves aren't level: They are taller in the center. So, **MOUND** the rest of the dirt on top of your gravesite.

8 Enjoy your neighbors' **ALARMED REACTIONS** to the zombie invasion. Don't hesitate to say, "Told you so!"

TIP: If you want a lusher lawn, this is a good opportunity to plant some grass seed. After you've surprised a sufficient number of neighbors, yank your zombie out of the earth and discard him, then plant some grass seed. Water regularly.

You Can't Keep a Good Pumpkin Down

Silly Epitaphs You Can Carve

I always say that a silly gravestone brings some fun to a funeral. Here are some zombie-appropriate gravestones to commemorate the undead in your front yard.

FESTER N. ROTT

He once was alive

But now he's not

WILLIE RIESAGIN

1908–1967–?

DEE KAYED

Here lies Dee, now food for worms

She didn't use soap and caught some germs

I TOLD YOU I WAS SICK!

BARRY M. DEEP

He'll rise again

When you're asleep

GIL A. TEEN

A-tisket, a-tasket

His head is in a basket

GET OFF OF ME!

CECIL B. FLATT

He was so brave

He was so cute

Until he forgot his parachute

IMA SINNER

Won't you join me?

BILL M. LATER

A simple man

Died of complications

JACK P. DRAKE

He hit the gas

Instead of the brake

Kiddie Candy Thief Alarm

Teach the kids there's no such thing as free candy. The bait will be a huge bowl of treats. To pull off the prank, you'll need noisemakers (sirens, whistles, a bullhorn, or a microphone and an amplifier), a spotlight or flashing or rotating lights, a power strip, and, of course, a good hiding place. Consider a bay window, some bushes, or the next-door neighbor's house.

THE SETUP

1. Plug all of your noises and lights into a single power strip. Position the strip so that you can turn it on easily from your hiding spot.

2. Place the giant bowl of candy on your front porch or wherever you normally would put it if you weren't home. Be sure it is well lit. Then turn off most of the lights inside your house so that it appears as if no one is home.

3. Show off your trap to your friends and neighbors. They will want to be in on the joke. Their laughter will also help keep the kids from bursting into tears when they are busted for candy theft.

4. Take your hiding spot and wait. It won't be long before you are flashing the sirens and lights on some wannabe candy thief.

5. You'll want to mix up your scares according to the age of the criminal—and how much candy the kid nabbed. Shouting "Stop! Candy thief!" with lights flashing is good for pint-size candy crooks. To create a more tactile surprise, turn on the lights and spray them with Silly String.

6. Give older, greedier kids the siren—they'll have a gratifying "guilty as charged" look on their faces. Helicopter sounds and a spotlight shining down from a tree will make grabby teenagers really nervous. (Why are they trick-or-treating anyway?) "Halt. Step away from the candy bowl" is the nail in the coffin.

Take One that is fair NO More or you'll get a SCARE!!

Talking Trashcan

Hiding in the bushes to scare trick-or-treaters used to be a common activity for dads. Unfortunately, in recent years, the goody-goodies have taken a lot of the fun out of Halloween and scaring kids isn't so popular. Because I don't have bushes in my yard, I developed this trick instead. If you want to become a Talking Trashcan, all you need is a big rubber trashcan with a lid, a jigsaw, and some rope and screws.

TRANSFORM YOUR TRASHCAN

1. ATTACH the lid to the trashcan with some 1-inch screws. This will make the trashcan more solid so you can ATTACK it with a jigsaw.

2. Next, use the jigsaw to SLICE OFF the bottom of the trashcan.

3. PLACE the trashcan over your head and determine where to make the head flap—that is, the TRAPDOOR that you can poke your head out of. SLICE three sides of the flap, but not the fourth side. It will act as a HINGE.

4. Put the trashcan over your head again and DETERMINE where the arm flaps need to be. You'll need a flap for each arm, starting from the tips of your fingers and extending to the tops of your shoulders. Again, SLICE three sides of each flap, leaving the top intact to act as a HINGE.

5. CUT two holes at the bottom of each arm flap and TIE a rope handle on each side. These handles will allow you to MANEUVER the flaps when you are inside the trashcan.

6. Try to CROUCH down while inside the trashcan. You probably won't be able to. If you can't, SLICE a back flap in the backside of the trashcan. This will allow you more FLEXIBILITY while you're hiding.

7. Ask AN ASSISTANT to help set you up in your trashcan costume. He or she can tell you if your arms or backside are POKING OUT.

8. Let trick-or-treaters walk past you to get their candy. POP out of the trashcan and scare them as they leave the house. SHOUT whatever you think a talking trashcan would say and wave your arms. The kids will LOVE it and so will you.

Killer Scorpion

DOES THE WORD "SCORPION" CONJURE VISIONS OF A DEADLY CREATURE FOR YOU— or an embarrassing heavy metal band from the '80s? Either way, you can be sure your neighbors will wish you didn't live nearby. This yard sculpture isn't difficult to build and it has visual presence. That means passersby will either want to take its picture or cross the street when approaching your house. Here is how to unleash the beast on your yard.

YOU'LL NEED:

- **CARVING TOOLS: jigsaw** (or pumpkin-carving saw), **router** (for removing gourd's skin), **drill with ⅝-inch bit** (electric or manual), and **mallet, hammer, or big rock** (in a pinch)

- **1 giant pumpkin** for thorax and abdomen (a flattish one is best)

- **1 large pumpkin** to create claws (a tall one is good)

- **1 gourd** that looks uncannily like a scorpion's head (the right pumpkin will work, too)

- **9 small(er) pumpkins** for the tail and arms

- **1 kettle gourd** with a bent neck for the stinger

- **One 6-foot-long piece of rebar** (steel reinforcement bar found at your local home center)

- **4 dried cornstalks**

Filet Your Critter

1. Using the jigsaw, **SLICE** the giant pumpkin in half from stem to bottom and back to the stem. This will be your scorpion's thorax (a scientific term for "torso" I am throwing around).

2. Take the large pumpkin and, using the reciprocating saw, **HACK** two big claws out of it. Try to **ENVISION** the last time you had crab, lobster, or crayfish, and think of those claws. It's cool if your claws are composed of broken pieces of pumpkin shell.

3 With the jigsaw and router, **SCULPT** the gourd to look like what you imagine the head of a scorpion to look like. Since scorpions have little heads, you will have to employ a bit of whimsy. I **SHAVED** giant bug eyes with a router and then used the gourd's stem for the snout. Do scorpion's have snouts?

Deploy the Stinger

4 **CHANNEL** Arnold Schwarzenegger and bend the rebar into a big arc. You will need to secure the bar under something to bend it (I used the two legs of my workbench), then **PULL, DON'T PUSH** on the bar. Wear gloves so you don't get slashed. It's not a difficult job, but you'll see, there's a certain satisfaction that comes from bending a big bar of metal.

5 **POUND** one end of the bent rebar into the ground. You'll need to drive it far enough in to hold up the weight of the tail (about 2 feet deep worked for my scorpion).

6 **CHOP OFF** the stems of five of the smaller pumpkins, then **DRILL** holes all the way through them, from stem end to bottom. Thread these pumpkins onto the rebar to create the tail.

7 **DRILL** a hole into the bottom of the gourd, but not all the way through. **THREAD** it on the rebar to top off the tail.

Arachnid Assembly

8 To create the thorax and abdomen, **LAY** the two cut halves of the giant pumpkin side by side. Both stem ends should face the same direction, and the tail should look like it's growing out of the abdomen segment.

9 Next, **POSITION** the scorpion's head at the top of the thorax.

10 **ARRANGE** the four remaining small pumpkins as segments of the arms: No carving required. **ADD** the claws.

11 To make the legs, start by **DRILLING** four holes along each side of the thorax and abdomen segments. The cornstalks will be placed in these holes, so angle the holes slightly upward to get a more realistic look.

12 Using the jigsaw, **CUT DOWN** the cornstalks to create four scorpion legs. Shave the tips off the stalks, and **PLUG** them into the holes in the thorax. **SPREAD OUT** the legs for a creepy, realistic effect. One giant lawn arachnid complete!

Unwelcome Visitors? Let Your Giant Scorpion Convey the Message

Motion-Sensor Scare Machine

We all would love to create a haunted house each year, but let's face it, that would be a major pain. If you have one of those motion-sensor porch lights, here is a trick that will get you big results for almost no work. Go to the hardware store and buy one of those things with an electric outlet on it that you can screw into a lightbulb socket. Put it in your motion-sensor lamp. Voilà! A motion-sensor electrical trigger. Plug one of the following appliances into your new scare machine and enjoy the show:

- **A STROBE LIGHT:** Nothing says "cool" like a motion-activated strobe light.

- **A BLACK LIGHT:** Especially if you still have your psychedelic posters from junior high, dude.

- **A CIRCULAR SAW OR OTHER NOISY POWER TOOL (WITH NO BLADE IN IT):** Even minus the blade, circular saws make a scary noise. So do reciprocating saws, jigsaws, Shop-Vacs, and grinders. Sanders and drills aren't so scary.

- **A LIGHT THAT ILLUMINATES A HIDDEN FIGURE:** Hide a camouflaged dummy in a tree or in your shrubs. When strangers approach and it is suddenly lit up, they'll freak out. Especially if that figure is wearing a hockey mask.

- **A CD PLAYER LOADED WITH SCARY SOUNDS:** Turn it up loud. I guarantee you'll never get tired of watching visitors jump out of their skins.

- **A LIVE VIDEO FEED OF YOUR PORCH:** Normally, people don't mind being on camera. In fact, they often ham it up. But on a gloomy Halloween night, seeing themselves can be quite frightening. Especially if the TV monitor is only visible through a dark window. I don't know about you, but I just love turning a safety device into something devious!

night, she purposefully kept her house as dark as possible so that kids wouldn't knock on her door. But no matter how dark she made the house, some kids would still knock. In fact, I bet that 25 percent of kids would walk up a completely dark pathway, climb onto a dark porch, and knock on the door of a completely darkened house if it might lead to free candy. This gag banks on it. Your porch will be lit and so will your walkway, but your door will be missing. In its place will be a black hole. When the kids approach . . . Boo! You'll get 'em!

YOU'LL NEED:

- **2 doorway-size closet rods** (the kind that use spring tension to stay up)

- **Measuring tape and scissors**

- **3 yards of the darkest black fabric you can find** (the heavier, the better)

- **A friend who can sew, a sewing machine, or a stapler or glue gun** (for slackers)

- **1 roll black duct tape**

- **A scary mask or an ugly face**

They Wanted a Treat But They Got Tricked Instead!

Rig Your Dark Doorway

1. If you have a storm door, **REMOVE** the glass.

2. **RIG** the closet rods across the very top and very bottom of your doorway. The rods will **HOLD** the dark fabric taut and in place. **MEASURE** the distance between the two rods. This will be the length of your **DARK CURTAINS**.

3. Cut and **SEW** (or **GLUE** or **STAPLE**) the fabric to create the curtain. (This is **REMEDIAL SEWING**. If I can do it, you can, too.)

4. **HANG** the curtain on the rods, then **CUT** a slit down the center of the curtain.

Get a Good Laugh

5. **POSITION YOURSELF** behind the curtain and shut it tightly. The curtain will not be easily visible until the kids get **TOO CLOSE**, then the gag will be fairly obvious.

6. For this reason, you will want to **SURPRISE THEM** as they approach. **POP OUT** of the slit in the curtain and **SHOUT** something brief. Don't get complex when one syllable is best (*Boo! Ahh! Rarrr!*). Mix up your scares: **STAND ON A STOOL** so that you appear very tall or **CROUCH DOWN** so you can attack them from below. Keep them guessing!

Creepy Candy Dispensers

Once you've scared the bejeezus out of your trick-or-treaters, invite them to help themselves to some candy. Here are some creative dispensers:

- **A TOILET BOWL:** Obviously, you'll need to buy a fresh one. Provide some tongs for grabbing the candy.

- **A TRASHCAN:** Mix some "trash" with the candy. Crumpled up newspapers and aluminum foil would complete the illusion.

- **A LITTER BOX:** Tootsie Rolls would be the perfect candy for this. No reason you can't throw in some sand and a stuffed kitten, too.

- **A WIG:** What could be less appetizing than grabbing food from a wig?

Zip-Line Ghost

IF YOU'VE EVER WATCHED *SCOOBY-DOO,* you know that the best tricks always involve ropes and pulleys. That is why I decided to incorporate them in this next haunt, the Zip-Line Ghost. You will construct your ghost out of papier-mâché (which is cheap and effective, though it takes a day to dry) and install him on a zip-line. Be ready with some awesome treats, though, because any kid brave enough to get past this ghoulish gatekeeper isn't going to be satisfied by those snack-size candy bars!

YOU'LL NEED:

FOR THE GHOST

- **Balloon** (and a pin to pop it)
- **Flour and water** (to make the papier-mâché goop)
- **Newspaper**
- **One 10-foot-long piece of PVC pipe** (plastic-vinyl pipes available at your local home center; I chose a 1½-inch-diameter pipe)
- **Handsaw** (to cut PVC pipe)
- **1 PVC tee**
- **1 PVC cross**
- **PVC pipe primer and cement** (also available at your local home center)
- **Utility knife**
- **Glue** (I used a hot-melt glue gun)

- **4 large zip ties**
- **1 rope pulley** (size should correspond to a ³⁄₈-inch-thick rope)
- **Drill with ¼-inch drill bit** (electric or manual)
- **White sheet** (I used a twin-size sheet)

FOR THE ZIP-LINE

- **2 large eye screws** (to thread the rope)
- **1 long, ³⁄₈-inch-thick piece of rope** (my rope was 75 feet long, but your length will depend on how far you want your ghost to travel)
- **1 rope cleat** (so you can control your ghost)
- **1 medium-size eye screw** (to attach the fishing line)
- **Fishing rod and reel with fishing line** (so you can reel your ghost in)

Make a Ghoulish Head

1. Start with the ghost's head since it will take about 24 hours for the papier-mâché to dry. **INFLATE** your balloon until it is the size you want for your ghost's head. If it **POPS**, make your ghost's head smaller or **BUY** some bigger balloons.

2. **COMBINE** 1 cup flour and 2 cups boiling water in a large bowl. **STIR** until it forms a smooth paste.

3. **TEAR** the newspaper into long strips. **DIP** the strips into the paste and wrap them around the balloon. (You did this in kindergarten when you made a piñata. It is fun.) **KEEP LAYERING** the strips until you have covered the balloon a few times.

4. After the paste is **DRY** (usually about one day), **POP** the balloon with a pin. Your ghost's head should feel solid. If it doesn't feel sturdy enough, **REPEAT** steps 2 and 3.

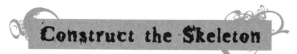

Construct the Skeleton

5. In "real" life ghosts may not have **SKELETONS**, but your zip-line ghost needs one. Take your PVC pipe and **SAW** off a 48-inch piece and an 18-inch piece. Saw the remaining PVC pipe **IN HALF** to create two pieces approximately 27 inches each.

6. Next **CREATE** a cross out of the four pieces of PVC pipe and the PVC cross piece, using the PVC primer and cement to **AFFIX** them together (see

instructions on the cans). The 48-inch piece will be the spine of your ghost, the 18-inch piece will be the neck, and the 27-inch pieces will form the arms.

7. When the PVC cement dries, in an hour or so, use a utility knife to **CUT** a hole in the bottom and top of the ghost's head, then slide it over the neck pipe. **GLUE** the head in place so that it will remain facing forward.

8. Using your PVC cement again, **AFFIX** the PVC tee to the neck piece; it should be positioned above the ghost's head and **PERPENDICULAR** to the arms. Use the zip ties to **ATTACH** the pulley so it sits above the tee. The entire ghost will hang from this pulley.

Dress Up the Ghost

9. **DRAPE** the sheet over the head of the ghost. Use a few dabs of glue to hold it in place, ensuring that the sheet will **STRETCH** to the tip of each arm. You can use some additional glue to **CREATE** some dramatic draping. Whether you are creating a ghost or hanging curtains, I always think dramatic draping makes all the difference!

Install the Zip-Line

10. **LOCATE** a high tree, post, or spot on your garage or house where you can hang something. Drill a ¼-inch hole in your spot and **INSTALL** one of the large eyehooks.

11 **FIND** a secure low spot, 50 to 75 feet from the high spot, and **INSTALL** another large eyehook. Be sure to pick a spot that will allow the ghost to **PASS** right by visitors, but not **DANGLE** in front of them. Nothing **RUINS THE FUN** like seeing the rope. Your rope should drop about 8 feet for every 20 feet it runs.

12 **TIE** the zip-line rope securely to the low eyehook. Don't ask me what kind of knot to use; I am not a Boy Scout. Just make sure it is **TIGHT**. Thread the rope through the pulley on your ghost, then **THREAD** the rope through the high eyehook. Hopefully your rope will still **REACH** the ground. If it doesn't, you'll need to **MOVE** one of your eyehooks closer to the other or **BUY** a longer rope.

13 **ATTACH** the rope cleat beneath the high spot (it should have come with screws). Next, pull the rope tight and **SECURE** it with the cleat. Rope cleats are great for people like me who aren't whizzes at knots. The cleat allows you to **CINCH** the rope tight and then **LET GO**. Hooray!

See If It Zips

14 You'll want to be sure your ghost actually **FLIES,** or you'll be very disappointed on Halloween night. Simply release the rope from the cleat and let your ghost **SLIDE** down the zip-line. If it doesn't slide easily, you'll need to pull your zip-line **TIGHTER** or mount it at a **STEEPER** angle.

15 Once the ghost is sliding with ease, **ATTACH** the small eyehook near the top of the zip-line. **THREAD** the fishing line through this eyehook and **TIE** it to the back of the ghost. You'll use the fishing line to **REEL** the ghost back up to the high point of the zip-line while you stand on the ground laughing.

Ropes and
Pulleys:
What Separates
the Halloween
Pros from
the Amateurs

Yard Serpent

DO YOU EVER WONDER how the truly wealthy celebrate Halloween? I don't. But I soon learned when I was asked to carve a pumpkin for a charity auction. The rich people were very nice, introducing me as a "bestselling author" and completely avoiding phrases like "doesn't have a trust fund." Then the auctioneer began the bidding. "Do I hear $300?" he asked. "Yeah, right," I thought. When the auction closed at one thousand bucks, I knew I was in deep trouble. I had twenty-four hours to create a pumpkin sculpture worth more than my first car, a 1982 Datsun. This giant Yard Serpent is what I came up with.

YOU'LL NEED:

FOR THE SKELETON

- **3 pieces rebar: 4 feet, 10 feet, and 6 feet long** (select ³⁄₈-inch-thick steel reinforcement bar, available at your local home center)

- **About 200 pounds heavy scrap metal** (I used old discs from a plow)

- **Welder** (to make this behemoth, you'll have to melt some metal)

- **4 tent stakes** (don't count on using them again)

- **One 1-foot-long piece metal tubing** (about 1¹⁄₂ inches in diameter)

- **Some serious brute strength** (and a helper or two)

FOR THE BODY AND FINS

- **30 to 40 small- to medium-size pumpkins for the body segments** (tall and skinny is the ideal shape)

- **1 large Hubbard squash** (these light green squash naturally look like serpents' heads)

- **CARVING TOOLS: reciprocating saw** (or keyhole saw), **drill with ³⁄₈-inch bit** (electric or manual), **mallet, hammer, or big rock** (if nothing else is handy), and a **big metal spoon** (or in this case, a shovel)

- **Drill with ³⁄₈-inch hole-cutting bit** (also known as a Forstner bit)

- **8 dried cornstalks** (where they sell pumpkins, they usually sell these)

- **1 roll dark-colored twine**

- **Pruning sheers**

Get Psyched

1. **LINE UP** all of your pumpkins, snake style: Biggest ones in the middle, smallest ones at the tip of the tail, and medium-size ones to form the neck. **HAVE A BEER**; this is going to be a long process.

2. **CLEAR THE YARD** of all small children, pets, or other creatures who might not be able to run fast enough to get out of the way of a **COLLAPSING SERPENT**.

3. **RECONSIDER** this project. (Unfortunately, I didn't have that luxury.)

Start with the Skeleton

4. You'll **FORM THE SKELETON** from the three lengths of rebar. Begin with **THE TAIL**, which is formed from the 4-foot-long piece of rebar. **BEND** it into a slight curve using all the strength you can muster. **WELD** one end of the arc to a heavy piece of scrap metal; this will keep the tail from falling over. (Keep in mind that you will have 30 to 40 pounds of pumpkins suspended in the air, so you need a wide, heavy base to anchor them.)

5. Move on to **THE NECK**. This is formed by bending the 6-foot-piece of rebar into a slight curve, then welding one end to a very heavy base. For added stability, **DRILL HOLES** through the base and **SECURE** it to the ground with some tent stakes.

6. **THE CENTER PIECE** is a challenge because it is a complete arc. This means that in order to string the pumpkins on it, you will have to make **TWO BASES**, one **REMOVABLE**. Bend the 10-foot-long piece of rebar into an arch, then weld a very heavy base on one end. To create a removable base for the other side, weld the foot-long piece of tubing to the other base; the free end of the rebar will rest in this tube. This should do the trick but it's a bit **UNWIELDY**. Handle with care.

Prepare Your Pumpkins

7. Handling the small- and medium-size pumpkins is easy enough. **CHOP** off the stems and **DRILL HOLES** all the way through, from stem end to base.

8. Using a reciprocating saw, **CARVE THE SERPENT'S HEAD** from the Hubbard squash. Give it some mean eyes and ferocious teeth. **DRILL** some nostrils. Finish by drilling a hole in the base of the head; don't drill all the way through.

Give Your Serpent Some Fins

9. To make sure the fins will **POINT UPWARD**, first figure out which side of the center arch is lightest—that will be the serpent's back. **DRILL** holes in the back where you want fins, then **JAB** a piece of cornstalk in each hole. Once you have a few cornstalks in place, give them all **A HAIRCUT** with some pruning sheers.

10. If you want, use leftover cornstalks to give your serpent **SOME FACIAL HAIR**. Drill some holes in the neck, **ADD** the cornstalks, and voilà—your serpent has a beard!

Shish Kebab Your Pumpkins

11 **DECIDE** where you want the serpent to go. Ideally, it will give the illusion of a serpent that is **SWIMMING IN THE DIRT** of your yard. Although you have made 20 feet of serpent, passersby will think there is much more of him **UNDERGROUND**.

12 Begin by constructing the tail, which is easiest to build. **STACK** the pumpkins on the tail, from biggest to smallest. After all of those pumpkins are on the armature, you'll see if the tail is **WOBBLY**. It if is, you will need to add more weight to the base.

13 Do the neck next. Start with **A REALLY HEAVY PUMPKIN** at the bottom of the rebar; you'll need it. **STACK** the rest of the pumpkins on top, from biggest to smallest, and finish with the head. Try to **JAB** the rebar into the head, as this will keep your serpent's head from flipping upside down.

Build a Bridge

14 The arch of the back is the most difficult to install. Lay the arch on its side, then **SLIDE** the pumpkins on the rebar. Once all the pumpkins have been **SHISH KEBABBED,** slide the free end of the rebar into the tube attached to the removable base.

15 Here's where you really need a **HELPER**. Carefully stand the entire arch up in **ONE MOTION**, taking care not to push it over to the other side. Determine if the arch is **STABLE**. If not, use the tent stakes and cord to secure it in position.

16 **CONGRATULATE** yourself: You've completed an expert-level pumpkin sculpture and your yard is definitely the coolest in the neighborhood. Any of the following **FINISHING TOUCHES** would make your Yard Serpent even cooler: aim **SPOTLIGHTS** on it, **STRING** holiday lights around it, **FOG IT UP** with dry ice dropped into a tub of water (or a fog machine), or give it **THREE HEADS** (two more pumpkins and some rebar will do the trick).

Look Who Showed Up Without an Invitation

A Coffin Full of Scares

WHAT EXACTLY DO COFFINS DO? Do they keep worms out, or simply keep dead flesh in? When I set out to make a coffin, I came up with my own criteria: It should be big enough for me, it should be easy to open so I can leap out and scare people, and, most important of all, it should be inexpensive as all heck. Wooden pallets make a great Old West–style pine box and they are free at the loading dock of any large store. You'll have to spring for a heap of deck screws, a couple hinges, and a half sheet of plywood, but these are small costs for a custom-made box of death.

YOU'LL NEED:

- **4 wooden pallets** (the pine ones you get for free at loading docks)

- **1 sheet plywood, about 7 feet by 28 inches** (you can make two coffins per sheet, one for you and one for your mate)

- **COFFIN-MAKING TOOLS: circular saw, cordless drill** (with a screwdriver bit), **ruler**, and **hammer or pry bar** (to dismantle the pallets)

- **About 100 deck screws** (I used 1³/₄-inch-long screws)

- **2 hinges** (big cheap ones)

- **A little bit of rope** (to make a handle for your coffin)

A Coffin Is Just a Box

1. **DISMANTLE** the pallets and remove the nails. This will be your **LUMBERYARD**.

2. You'll cut out the back panel of the coffin first. **SKETCH** a coffin shape on the plywood, using a ruler to make sure the two sides match. **LIE DOWN** on the template to make sure you'll **FIT COMFORTABLY** in the coffin. If everything checks out, **CUT** along the lines using a circular saw.

3. **MEASURE** the long side of one side of the coffin. Using the circular saw, **CUT** a piece of pallet wood to the same length and nail it into place with some deck screws.

4. **REPEAT** step 3 for the remaining three sides of the coffin (the other long side and the two short sides). Your box of death is starting to take shape.

5 **MEASURE** the width of one piece of pallet lumber. **SAW** six reinforcement boards so they are four times as long. **INSTALL** these boards in each of the corners of the coffin with some deck screws.

6 **MEASURE** the length of each edge of your coffin, then **CUT** four pieces of pallet lumber to build up each edge. **NAIL** these pieces to the reinforcement boards with more deck screws to build up the side of your coffin. After four rounds, your coffin should be **COMPLETE**.

Give Your Casket Some Doors

7 Here's how to create what I'd call a **DUTCH DOOR**, which will allow you to open the top or bottom of the coffin separately for **DRAMATIC EFFECT**.

8 The coffin doors will need to be the **SAME SIZE** as the back of the coffin. So, **TURN** the coffin over and **ARRANGE** a series of boards on top. **OUTLINE** the shape of the coffin on the boards and, using a saw, **CUT** the planks along the outline.

9 Use some scraps of pallet lumber and deck screws to **JOIN** all of these planks together (see photo for ideas). You will now have a single large coffin door. **ADD** a little more reinforcement, then **SAW** the door in two so you have a **BOTTOM DOOR** (that will reveal your feet and legs) and a **TOP DOOR** (that will reveal your torso and head).

10 Hinging the doors is important, but I was too cheap and **SLOPPY** to do it elegantly. I just bought some **CRUDDY STEEL HINGES** at the home center and **SCREWED** them in. To **PREVENT** the doors from opening too far, screw pieces of rope from the inside of the coffin to the inside of each door.

Rest in Peace?

11 If you want to rest in peace, you could **LINE** the inside of the coffin with some nice velveteen fabric and comfy padding, but let's be honest, this coffin is supposed to look a little **BEAT-UP** and **GRUNGY**. The interior of mine went **UNFINISHED**.

It'll Make a Quaint Flower Box When Springtime Arrives

Creepy Things to Do with a Coffin

As if having a beaten-up, "home on the range" kind of coffin sitting in your front yard weren't scary enough, here are some super-creepy touches you can add to your death box to ensure maximum scare factor. Note: If you plan to hide in a coffin full of candy, be sure to eat a good dinner first, or you may find yourself in a coffin full of barf.

- **HIDE IN THE COFFIN.** Surprise anyone who comes close. Don't feel bad; you are not being underhanded in any way. Trick-or-treaters who see a coffin in a yard should assume that there is someone inside it.

- **PUT CANDY IN THE COFFIN.** I've realized that the more kids I scare off, the more candy I get to keep. Forcing the kids to open up a strange and dirty-looking coffin to get their candy is a sure-fire way to keep *your* sugar buzz running until Thanksgiving.

- **FOG IT UP.** If you happen to own a fog machine, I suggest that you place it inside the coffin. If your coffin isn't intimidating enough, it will be when fog starts pouring out of it.

- **BURY IT A LITTLE BIT.** You may not want to dig up your yard at Halloween, but you can mound a bunch of leaves around your coffin to give it that subterranean look.

- **CREATE A FALSE BOTTOM IN YOUR COFFIN.** Use some heavy black fabric; it will allow you to burst through whenever someone opens the hatch. You could even stand the coffin up vertically on your porch and hide behind the false bottom. Whenever kids open it up— boom! You get them.

Baby-Eating Yard Monster

I AM ALWAYS EXCITED when I get my hands on a giant pumpkin. Unfortunately, I have squandered the opportunity in the past by carving a Jabba the Hutt that no one recognized and a morbidly obese troll. This time, I shelled out additional dough for a bunch of smaller pumpkins. This excess is sure to impress, even if your carving does not. I call this one the Baby-Eating Yard Monster because he looks like he could snarf a toddler or two in one bite. In fact, turn the page and you will see him doing just that!

YOU'LL NEED:

- **CARVING TOOLS: reciprocating saw** (or keyhole saw), **drill with 3/8-inch bit** (electric or manual), **angle grinder** (for flaying the pumpkin's skin), **mallet, hammer, or big rock** (if nothing else is handy), and a **big metal spoon** (or in this case, a shovel)

- **1 giant pumpkin for the body** (mine weighed in at 200 pounds)

- **12 small pumpkins for the legs**

- **4 medium-size pumpkins for the claws** (tall and narrow ones are best)

- **Two 4-foot-long pieces of rebar** (steel reinforcement bar found at your local home center)

- **1 baby onesie stuffed with old rags, optional** (a onesie is a one-piece baby outfit, pronounced "won-zee")

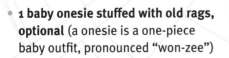

Monsterous Expressions

1. **SCALP** the giant pumpkin and **SCOOP OUT** all of his guts with a big metal spoon. This is a messy job—you may want to enlist some gullible children to assist.

2. Using the reciprocating saw, **CARVE** a hideous monster face on the giant pumpkin. (You could try using a keyhole saw, but for pumpkin flesh of this magnitude, a power tool is your best bet.) Give your monster **PLENTY OF FANGS**, but carve the top and bottom fangs so they are continuous (see photo) or your giant pumpkin could collapse. Use the angle grinder to **SHAVE** the pumpkin skin off of the fangs so they look more realistic.

Give Him Some Arms

3 Choose where you want the upper arms to attach to the giant pumpkin. **DRILL** two holes to **MARK THE SPOTS**.

4 **BEND** the two pieces of rebar so they look like **THRASHING ARMS**. (You will need to secure each bar under something heavy in order to bend it, then **PULL, DON'T PUSH** on the bar. Wear gloves.) **SHOVE** one piece of rebar into each hole, then using a mallet, **POUND** them all the way through the pumpkins and **INTO THE DIRT** below. This will hold the rebar steady.

5 **CHOP** off the stems of six small pumpkins, then **DRILL HOLES** all the way through them, from stem end to base. **THREAD** them on the rebar, three pumpkins per arm.

Watch Out! He Has Claws

6 Using the reciprocating saw, **HACK** clawlike appendages out of the four medium-size pumpkins. If you need to buy and **EAT A LOBSTER** for inspiration, do so.

7 **THREAD** two of the claws on the ends of the rebar to complete the upper arms.

8 **POSITION** two of the claws on the ground in front of the pumpkin, so they look really menacing. **ARRANGE** the remaining six small pumpkins on the ground between the giant pumpkin and claws to create the front legs. Your monster is **READY FOR ACTION!**

9 If you have a twisted sense of humor, then you'll want to add this **SICK FINISHING TOUCH**. Thrust the baby onesie into the monster's month, so it looks like the baby is being **GOBBLED UP, HEADFIRST**. I propped up one leg of the onesie with a stick. This will create the illusion that the baby is actually struggling as it is being eaten.

10 **AWAIT THE PHONE CALLS** from irate neighbors who object to your monster's mini meal.

Keep Your Children and Pets Close

Make Your Own Fake Blood

I use a lot of fake blood and I am cheap. Therefore, I don't buy fake blood: I make it myself. Here's how you can make some, too.

YOU'LL NEED:

- 4 tablespoons cornstarch
- $\frac{1}{2}$ cup cold water
- One 32-ounce bottle corn syrup (4 cups)
- About 20 drops red food coloring
- About 20 drops blue food coloring
- An empty 2-liter soda bottle (or other container to store your blood)
- A funnel (to get this sticky liquid into your storage container)

Blood on a Budget

1. Using a fork or whatever else you have handy, mix the cornstarch and cold water in a cereal bowl until the cornstarch has dissolved.

2. In a large pan over medium heat, combine the corn syrup and the cornstarch mixture, stirring until well mixed. Swirl in the red and blue food coloring, a few drops a time, until you achieve the color of blood (or at least the color of fake blood in horror movies).

3. When the mixture comes to a boil, turn off the heat and remove it from the burner. Let it cool, stirring occasionally.

4. When your fake blood is completely cool, pour it into the empty soda bottle and screw on the cap securely. It is super sticky (and attracts flies once it's out of the bottle), but it will keep for well over a year.

TIP: If you want to dribble some of this blood into your yard monster's mouth (or onto the struggling victim), transfer it to a squeeze bottle, like those TV chefs do.

Scary Scarecrow

THIS PARTICULAR GAG is amazingly simple and yet it is so effective. You disguise yourself in a scarecrow costume and frighten people who venture onto your porch. I'll give you some tips on making the scarecrow gag as believable as possible, but even a lazy man can get a big response with this prank.

YOU'LL NEED:

- **Scarecrow costume complete with a mask** (you can buy a full costume, as shown here, or use old clothes, gloves, boots, and a mask)

- **Heaps of leaves from your yard** (to stuff the scarecrow)

- **Bench or chair** (to position near your front door)

- **A willing accomplice** (to give out the candy)

- **Lots of patience** (and the desire to frighten the clueless)

Method One: The Easy Way

1. **DRESS UP** in your scarecrow costume and **SIT STILL** on your front porch.

2. When someone approaches, **DON'T MOVE.** They will likely be distracted by the candy being given out. **WAIT** them out.

3. When the time is right, **SCARE** the high-fructose corn syrup out of them!

Method Two: Be Thorough

1. On October 1 or thereabouts, **MAKE** a scarecrow using all of your supplies and **SIT** him or her on your porch. Your neighbors will get used to seeing him there. Be sure that he has **FULL COVERAGE** (mask, gloves, and boots), and that he is around **YOUR SIZE**. Stuff him so full of leaves that he sits upright.

2. On Halloween, **DISMANTLE** the scarecrow and **PUT ON** all of its clothes. **REPEAT** steps 2 and 3 of the easy method, above.

THE SCARECROW

ME POSING AS THE SCARECROW

Sometimes
the Most
Obvious Gag
Is the
Creepiest

8 Steps to the Perfect Scare

1. **DECIDE IN ADVANCE WHO IS GOING TO BE SCARED.** It is a solid line, not a fuzzy one. Some visitors will get no action, others are going to get the full scare. I scare anyone old enough to have abandoned the silly candy container their mom gave them. If you are holding a pillowcase, you are going to get it.

2. **THERE IS NO SUCH THING AS A HALF-SCARE.** An uncommitted monster is not scary.

3. **THERE IS NO MINIMUM DISTANCE FROM WHICH TO SCARE SOMEONE.** Some people won't be paying attention; you should let them get as close as possible.

4. **THERE IS A MAXIMUM DISTANCE.** If you try to surprise someone from too far away, you'll simply blow your cover. Figure out the maximum distance, and don't start before your victim gets closer than that.

5. **THE SCARE SHOULD HAPPEN AS SUDDENLY AS POSSIBLE.** It is not slow. It is not gentle. You will need to move suddenly and make a bunch of noises at the same time. Think of something scary to scream, even if it is just "RAH!" Don't try to say anything specific; people will be too surprised to comprehend what you're trying to say.

6. **MOVE IN CLOSER.** A scare is scarier if you invade someone's personal space and fill their field of vision.

7. **SCARE THE PERSON CLOSEST TO YOU.** If there is a group, that person will jump back and startle the other members of the group. The effect will be like dominos—frightened dominos that pee their pants, that is.

8. **NEVER APOLOGIZE.** If you scare them to death, they'll get over it. If you think they were terrified but they weren't, apologizing will make you look like an egotistical jerk.

Flaming Pumpkin Tiki Torches

YOU CAN FIND TIKI TORCHES IN EVERY MEGA STORE. Unfortunately, none of them actually looks like a tiki. I guess if they were called "wicker basket torches," no one would buy them. You, my friend, do not have to settle for subpar tikis as your torches. You can carve a few pumpkins to actually look like tiki heads, then light up your yard. That way, your guests are sure to know where the party is.

NOTE: Don't mess around! Your garden hose won't put out a kerosene fire. Keep a fire extinguisher (type ABC) at the ready.

YOU'LL NEED:

- **3 or more large pumpkins** (as big as the head of a giant Samoan)
- **CARVING TOOLS: jigsaw** (or pumpkin-carving saw), **router or Dremel rotary tool** (or chisel), **drill and drill bits** (electric or manual), **big metal spoon**, plus **dry-erase markers in two colors** (to draw your designs before you carve)
- **A fire extinguisher** (type ABC)
- **Toilet paper** (at least one roll per pumpkin)
- **An aluminum baking dish or other shallow pan** (disposable or previously damaged is best)
- **1 gallon kerosene** (available at your local home center, usually near the portable heaters or in the paint department)
- **Tongs** (or really big pliers)
- **Long fireplace matches** (or one of those long-handled grill lighters)
- **Some idea of what a tiki actually looks like** (check out some online photos before you begin)

Carve Your Tikis

1. Using a jigsaw, **SCALP** your pumpkins, discarding the tops, then **GUT** them with a big metal spoon. You don't have to do a thorough job, but you will need to remove most of the goop.

2. **DRAW** your tiki designs on the pumpkins in **TWO COLORS**. One color should represent the area you will **CUT AWAY** completely; the other area should represent where you will simply **PEEL AWAY** the skin.

3 CARVE your pumpkins and **FLAY** their skin. **KEEP AT IT** until the work is done. Even using power tools, a tiki design is complicated and can take more than 30 minutes to complete. Carving them all at once is **MORE EFFICIENT**, because you won't spend as much time switching between your jigsaw, router, and drill.

Get Set . . .

4 Place the **TOILET PAPER** in the shallow pan, one roll per pumpkin. **POUR** kerosene over the TP until every roll is soaked through. There should be a little **UNABSORBED KEROSENE** in the bottom of the pan. Let the toilet paper **SOAK** for a few more minutes, and then **ADD MORE** kerosene if you think it will be absorbed.

5 POSITION your pumpkins along your **WALKWAY OR ON A PATIO**, far away from **ANYTHING FLAMMABLE**. They should not be on or near any dried leaves, low-hanging vegetation, or **STRUCTURES OF ANY KIND**. These pumpkins will have flames shooting out of the top of them, so once they are **LIT**, keep an eye on yourself, your property, and especially **ANY KIDS** in the vicinity. I know I shouldn't have to say this to people that are smart enough to read a book, but don't even **THINK** about lighting your tiki pumpkins indoors.

6 Using the tongs, **PLACE** a roll of kerosene-soaked toilet paper in each pumpkin. **CHECK CAREFULLY** to be sure no kerosene is dripping out of any of the pumpkins.

7 Reaching through the mouths of the pumpkins (never from above!), **LIGHT** each roll of toilet paper. The flames should reach their peak after about 2 minutes and last for 30 to 60 minutes. **AWWWW, YEAH!** After the flames die and the insides go cold, you can throw them away.

When We Say "Aloha," We Mean "Happy Halloween"

Painfully Obvious Fire-Safety Tips

The fact that you have survived long enough to read this book suggests that you may not need these tips. But you can never be sure, so I'll proceed.

- **DON'T LIGHT YOURSELF ON FIRE.** People stumble upon all sorts of creative ways of doing this, like putting their hand in the kerosene and then using the same hand to strike a match. Don't do this, or anything else that may cause you to ignite.

- **IF YOU DO MAKE A FIRE, STICK AROUND TO WATCH IT.** Not only are flames cool to look at but they also need supervision. Don't leave them untended, even for a second or two. Don't.

- **KEEP A FIRE EXTINGUISHER HANDY.** It needs to be capable of putting out the type of fire you have burning: a type ABC can put out kerosene fires. The fire extinguisher also needs to be full; otherwise it is not a fire extinguisher, it is an empty bottle.

- **KEEP FLAMMABLE THINGS AWAY FROM THE FIRE.** Fires like to spread, but they don't spread by magic. They spread from one flammable thing to another, which you can prevent by making sure that the next flammable thing is too far away to catch fire. (Note: This is easier to accomplish if you remove all flammable stuff before you light the fire.)

- **KEEP ANYONE DUMBER THAN YOU AWAY FROM THE FIRE.** That should be just about everyone because I know that you are really smart. You did, after all, buy this great work of literature.

- **KEEP KIDS AWAY FROM THE FIRE.** Kids deserve every break they can get, and you are going to give them one here by looking out for them. Keep them safe until they are at least old enough to drive themselves to the hospital.

Halloween Hangman

WHY NOT CELEBRATE HALLOWEEN the way I think they would have done it in the Old West—with a good old-fashioned hanging? Of course, in my imagination, back then they would have drawn straws to see which guy would sacrifice his life to become the town's most gruesome Halloween decoration. In our case, we already know the pumpkin will be the victim. Or actually, the Funkin: I rarely use a fake pumpkin, but in this case I recommend using one for its light weight.

YOU'LL NEED:

- **Four 8-foot-long 2x4s for the gallows** (that's 32 feet of lumber total)

- **Miter saw**

- **Drill with a screw bit** (or a screwdriver)

- **About 25 deck screws** (2½-inch-long ones are ideal)

- **1 large eyehook** (you'll run the rope through this)

- **15 feet of noose-quality rope** (go for the thick, gnarly-looking stuff)

- **Noose-tying instructions** (look them up online or in a handy knot-tying guide)

- **Fake pear-shaped pumpkin** (found at craft or party stores)

- **Jigsaw** (or pumpkin-carving saw)

- **Fake skeleton** (unless you have a real one lying about)

- **Glue** (I used a hot-melt glue gun)

- **Zip ties**

- **Stool, orange crate, or old chair** (for the hanging man to jump off)

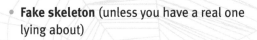

A Little Gallows Humor

1. Let's start by building the gallows. **SAW** two 8-foot 2x4s in half. You will **CONSTRUCT** the base from three of these pieces and the top of the gallows from the remaining piece. To make the base solid, simply **SCREW** the three pieces of wood into a big I shape. **NO PROBLEM**, right?

2. Using deck screws, **ATTACH** the base of the gallows to the remaining 2x4.

3. To keep the post from **WOBBLING**, use the miter saw to make **FOUR ANGLED SUPPORTS**. It really

How's It Hanging?

doesn't matter how long the supports are. Just be sure to **SAW** the ends at a 45-degree angle, then use the deck screws to attach one support at the top of the gallows and three at the base (as shown in photo).

4 Before you **INSTALL** the top of the gallows, insert the eyehook. **DRILL** a pilot hole about 1 foot from one end. **SCREW** in the eyehook.

5 **INSTALL** the top of the gallows, using your fourth support bar to **STABILIZE** it. You should be able to **STAND** the entire contraption up now.

Tie and Hang the Noose

6 The traditional hangman's noose **LOOPS** 13 times. Yours should, too. Following the instructions you've looked up online, **TIE** an evil-looking noose.

Craft Your Halloween Victim

7 Using a jigsaw, **CARVE** your craft-store pumpkin so it looks like a skull. Your pumpkin died an **UNTIMELY DEATH,** so you should give him a corresponding expression.

8 Next **REMOVE** the head of your skeleton and **CINCH** the noose around its neck.

9 To attach the pumpkin skull to the body, **DRILL** a hole in the base of the pumpkin skull and **STUFF** the top vertebrae in the hole. To make the connection more secure, use the jigsaw to **HACK** a notch from the back of the skull and **GLUE** the noose to the vertebrae. (You'll discover that the quality of Halloween store skeletons is **DUBIOUS** at best. Zip ties come in handy when the arms, almost inevitably, **FALL OFF.** And a glue gun will be useful in multiple instances.)

Hang 'Em

10 To hang your skeleton, **THREAD** the loose end of the rope through the eyehook, **HOIST** your victim in place, and **KNOT** the rope securely around the uppermost support bar. (You may need an executioner's assistant for this step.) Position the stool (or crate or chair) beneath the victim, **OUT OF REACH** of his toes.

11 **WAIT** to see what happens. Less than 24 hours after staging my execution, the police **KNOCKED** on my door. You see, I had executed my Halloween hangman in mid-November and the neighbors didn't find it very **FUNNY.**

Famous Last Words

I suspect that on my deathbed I will say something stupid like, "I shouldn't have eaten all those fish tacos," or something similarly mundane. But I will cross my fingers that I have the presence of mind to steal these famous last words from one of the greats instead.

- "Go on, get out. Last words are for fools who haven't said enough."
  —political philosopher Karl Marx

- "I just wish I had time for one more bowl of chili."
  —frontiersman Kit Carson

- "I hope I haven't bored you."
  —crooner Elvis Presley

- "Don't let it end like this. Tell them I said something."
  —Mexican revolutionary Pancho Villa

- "I knew it. I knew it. Born in a hotel room—and God damn it—died in a hotel room."
  —playwright Eugene O'Neill

- "I am still alive."
  —Roman emperor Gaius Caligula

- "Shoot straight, you bastards! Don't make a mess of it!"
  —Australian folk hero Henry Morant to his firing squad

- "Now, now, my good man, this is no time for making enemies."
  —writer/philosopher Voltaire, when asked by a priest to renounce Satan

EXTREME PARTY TRICKS

THROW AN OUTRAGEOUS HALLOWEEN PARTY

The second half of this book is devoted to tricks you can play on trick-or-treaters and other Halloween guests. You're on your own turf so you have the home-field advantage: We'll teach you how to surprise your visitors at every turn. We'll also teach you the best ways to disgust your friends. From appetizers to the main course and dessert, every bite will have the power to nauseate. Even a trip to the bathroom won't be safe in your house.

Costumes are always a point of contention. The creative types like you and me never seem to have a problem, but some heel is always showing up to the party without proper attire. We'll show them because I'll also cover some crazy costumes you can spring on an unprepared guest. So read on and have fun. It is Halloween party time.

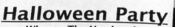

Halloween Party

Where: The Nardone's
When: Saturday, Oct. 30th
Time: 7:00 PM – Dawn
What to bring: Kids, Pumpkins
RSVP: 586-214-5964

costumes are mandatory

Anatomically Correct Invitations

I FIGURE there are a few too many Halloween party invitations featuring ghosts and pumpkins, so I make mine from an old anatomy book. I stick a big, blank, white sticker on the back of the gross picture I want to use. Then I cut the picture out of the book using an X-Acto knife or scissors, write up my invite, and send it off. The gross imagery let's people know my party will be something unusual. If you can't find an old anatomy textbook, look for some other book of weird imagery, such as old horror movie posters or photos of crime-scene investigations.

YOU'LL NEED:

- **Old book containing gross pictures** (you must be willing to destroy it)

- **1 package of large white stick-on labels** (I used 4x6-inch ones)

- **An X-Acto knife, scissors, or a box cutter** (the box cutter may be overkill)

- **Envelopes** (be sure to cut your invites to fit)

- **Pen or marker** (choose one that won't smudge)

Cut and Paste Your Way to These Gutsy Invitations

Time to Slash and Stick

1. Open your book and **SELECT** a gross picture. **TURN** the page over and **STICK** a label on the other side.

2. Flip back to the **CREEPY PICTURE** you picked and cut it out with your sharp tool of choice. You'll end up with the picture on the front and a plain white back. **ALTERNATIVELY,** you can just stick your label on the front of your picture; your guests don't need to see all of the **NASTY BITS**.

3. **WRITE** the event details and RSVP info on the back. If you have bad penmanship, type it up and print it on the label before you stick it on the invite in step 1.

4. **STUFF** the invite in an envelope and address it. **REPEAT** steps 1 through 4 until you run out of friends.

Funny Costumes You Already Own

If you're like me, you like to think of a new costume every Halloween. Some years, you come up with the perfect idea in March. Other years, you can barely coax your lazy self to take a trip to the closet. If this is one of those years, let me help. Here are a bunch of easy costumes that you already own:

- **THAT TRENDY PERSON, CIRCA 15 YEARS AGO:** Dig out your oldest clothes, the ones that you wouldn't be caught dead wearing today. Put together the most outrageous mix of them and you are done. Bonus points if you still own the shoes (and remember how to do your hair) to match. Check out my tracksuit and sweatband ensemble in the photos above.

- **A PROFESSIONAL:** This worked for the Village People, so why not for you? You probably have some clothes that resemble another person's profession. Here are some ideas:

  - Farmer (jeans, suspenders, flannel shirt, baseball cap)
  - Plumber (suspenders, plunger, pants too low in the back)
  - Cop (dark blue or black clothes and a badge made from aluminum foil)
  - Butcher (a meat cleaver and a bloody white apron—we all have one of those!)
  - Electronics-Store Clerk (blue oxford shirt, khaki pants, name tag)
  - Lunch lady (dirty white smock, a large spoon, a larger mole, and a hairnet)
  - Fishmonger (a rain coat and smelly fish guts)
  - The Makeup Counter Lady (lots of makeup, a perfume atomizer, white lab coat)
  - Nursery School Worker (disheveled clothes with bits of food, toys, and diapers attached)

- **A CATERPILLAR:** Climb into your sleeping bag and add some aluminum foil antennae. A great costume to wear to a cold, outdoor party. (Of course, you won't be able to dance and move about very well; the hopping gets exhausting.)

- **A GHOST:** You really can't go wrong with this classic. You need a white sheet, but I am sure you have one of those. If you don't have a white sheet, you cannot use a *Star Wars* sheet. If you are looking to take this costume one step further, take inspiration from *It's the Great Pumpkin, Charlie Brown!* and draw a bunch of black spots on the sheet. (Remember Charlie Brown had a little trouble positioning the holes for his eyes?)

Trashy Costumes for the Unprepared Guest

Some dodos never seem to figure out the meaning of a "costume" party. Every Halloween, they show up dressed in their regular clothes. Not only are they not participating, but they often have an air of smug superiority as they flout the very premise of the party. Well, this year, it's payback time. Insist that your uncooperative guest wear a costume made from everyday household items. Next year, he won't forget to dress up like the rest of us.

- **TOILET PAPER MUMMY:** It only takes a few minutes to make a great costume and a toilet paper mummy is one. Sure, it will be ruined in an hour, but what fun it will be until then. Take your guest aside and start wrapping him. Don't stop until he looks foolish. One roll of TP should do the job.

- **CARDBOARD BOX ROBOT:** Save some big cardboard boxes. You can paint them silver, or not. You can apply aluminum foil, or not. You can precut the arm and leg holes with a razor blade, or not. (Note: Doing the cutting in front of your scofflaw guest will help reinforce your new zero-tolerance policy.)

- **OLD BLANKET BURRITO:** Don't throw away that old wool blanket; use it to swaddle your unprepared guest like a delicious Mexican-food favorite. First, wrap him up tightly, securing the blanket with some duct tape. Use scissors to cut a hole for his face (he may be an annoying freeloader, but you don't want to smother him), and some arm holes, so he can have a drink. Send him on his merry way. He'll figure out how to deal with going to the bathroom when the time comes.

- **GARBAGE BAG BALLERINA:** You can make a tutu in minutes using some trash bags and a roll of masking tape. As you wrap the tape around your subject, bunch the kitchen bags around her waist. Finish the fun with more tape: corset her ribcage, make her sleeves puffy, and strap tape in spirals around her calves to create a pair of ribbony ballet shoes. Works equally well for male guests.

- **NEWSPAPER MUSCLE MAN:** This idea, like the one above, works for both men and women who show up unprepared, but I prefer this one for the guys. Using whatever clothes he came in, just wad up a bunch of newspaper and stuff it inside his shirt and pants. Stuff tons of it around the biceps, pecs, and lats, and don't forget the quads and glutes. Pump them up! Don't stop until he looks ridiculous. A three-pound dumbbell is the perfect accessory.

Extreme Pumpkin-Carving Table

AS THE AUTHOR OF TWO BESTSELLING PUMPKIN-CARVING BOOKS, you know that I take my pumpkin carving seriously. Well, you know wrong, because I don't. I'll carve a pumpkin anywhere: on a rock, in a sock, on a dock, while wearing a smock. But when I am throwing a pumpkin-carving party, I like to create the perfect conditions. This pumpkin-carving table has it all—individual pumpkin-carving stations complete with tool holders, power outlets, receptacles for refuse, and a place to secure the pumpkins while your guests carve. The table is also completely recyclable. When Halloween is over, take it apart and build something else.

YOU'LL NEED:

- **2 sawhorses or filing cabinets** (to set the tabletop on)

- **1 large sheet of plywood** (it should be at least 1/2-inch thick)

- **Three 2x4s** (at least 8 feet long)

- **Buckets or trash bags** (for pumpkin guts)

- **TOOL KIT: jigsaw, electric drill** (with a Phillips bit), **deck screws, router or electric sander** (optional; to round off the edges of the tabletop)

- **Paint and paintbrush** (optional; if you want to add some color)

PUMPKIN-CARVING STATIONS

- **PUMPKIN-CARVING TOOLS: jigsaw** (or pumpkin-carving saw), **electric drill** (or handheld one), **a chef's knife** (to carve details), and **a big metal spoon** (for removing pumpkin guts)

- **Power strips** (if you're providing power tools)

- **Painter's dropcloth** (enough to create a 4-foot-square buffer zone around each carver)

Build a Better Table

1. **MEASURE** the width of your sawhorses and the length of your plywood. **BUILD** a rectangle out of the 2x4s that is at least 1 inch wider than the sawhorses and shorter than the length of the plywood.

2 **SCREW** the rectangle together with deck screws and the electric drill, then screw the rectangle to the plywood tabletop. This will **STIFFEN** the tabletop and keep it from sliding off the sawhorses.

3 **ASK** an assistant to help you lift the tabletop onto the sawhorses. See how stable and nice it is! **WELL DONE.**

Add the Bells and Whistles

4 **SAW** three holes in the top of the table: one for pumpkin guts, one for trash, and one for recyclables. **POSITION** a bucket or trash bag under each one.

5 To create individual **PUMPKIN-CARVING STATIONS**, saw some triangles with rounded corners about 8 inches long out of the tabletop. Each will **HOLD** a pumpkin securely while it is being carved.

6 To make holders for pumpkin-carving tools, **DRILL** some holes near each pumpkin-carving station. **TAKE IT EASY** though, Sparky: If you cut too much stuff out of your sheet of plywood, there will be nothing left to hold it together.

7 If you want to scale it up, use an electric sander to **ROUND** the edges of the tabletop. **PAINT** the table with some cool designs.

8 **INVITE** your friends over for a pumpkin-carving party. **SET UP** a pumpkin-carving station for each of them, complete with 4-square feet of dropcloth, a set of pumpkin-carving tools, and a pumpkin or two. Let the **GOOD TIMES** roll.

9 When the party's over, cleanup will be easy. **EMPTY** the trash receptacles. **CLEAN** the carving tools and put them away. **GRAB** all four corners of each piece of dropcloth, **WRAP** up the pumpkin guts, and **TOSS** the cloth. **DISASSEMBLE** the table and **RECYCLE** the parts.

TIP: After exhaustive experimentation with 14 different cleaning solutions, I've discovered the best way to **PRESERVE CARVED PUMPKINS**. Cover the surface of your pumpkin with a bathroom cleaner containing bleach. The bleach seems to kill any mold and bacteria, while the cleaner keeps the bugs and squirrels away.

Behold the Pumpkin-Carving Table!

Pumpkin Pranks

Each year guests at our pumpkin-carving party commit a serious error in judgment. By letting me supply them with pumpkins, they save themselves time and trouble, but they also leave their pumpkins in my care. That gives me the chance to fill the pumpkin with evil surprises. Sometimes I cut a hole in the pumpkin, fill it up, and then glue the hole shut. Other times, I fill the pumpkin using a marinade injector from the cooking supply store. Below are some disgusting pumpkin fillers to consider.

POSSIBLE PUMPKIN FILLERS

- Fake blood (see recipe, page 41)
- Pennies
- Candy corn
- Slime
- Grease
- Caramel sauce
- Chocolate syrup
- Something stinky (like Vietnamese fish sauce)
- Whipped cream
- Maraschino cherries
- Olives
- Live crickets or meal worms
- Creamed corn, baked beans, or chili
- Already roasted pumpkin seeds

Make a Prank Pumpkin

1. TURN the pumpkin upside down and FIND an inconspicuous place to make a hole.

2. CARVE the smallest hole possible, being sure to PRESERVE the plug.

3. FILL the pumpkin with pennies, chocolate sauce, crickets, or other filling of your choice from the above list.

4. USE wood glue to REATTACH the plug right where you pulled it out.

5. ALLOW the glue to dry thoroughly. SMUDGE some dirt on the pumpkin to HIDE your incision.

6. PLAY your prank—and do it soon, or you may have spoiled whipped cream or dead crickets to contend with. I prefer to prank folks who are young or squeamish or both.

The Haunted Lavatory

Here's an interesting fact to consider: Chances are good that every guest at your party will go to the bathroom at some point during the festivities. When they do, they will (usually) be alone. That's why it's fun to haunt your bathroom. In fact, why not make it the scariest room in your house? People will really enjoy silly (even downright stupid) gags when you put them in the bathroom. Here are ideas to make a visit to your bathroom creepy and fun:

- **BOOBY-TRAPPED MEDICINE CABINET:** Some people can't resist looking in the medicine cabinet. That's why I load mine up with marbles. Hold the marbles in place using a piece of cardboard. After closing the cabinet door, slip the cardboard out. The next person that opens the medicine cabinet will create a racket almost as embarrassing as my personal stash of hemorrhoid creams.

- **FLICKER FLAME LIGHTS IN THE VANITY:** These are an oddity you can find at most home centers. They are lightbulbs that look like flickering flames. They screw into regular outlets. Try replacing your vanity bulbs with them for a spooky look.

- **SOAP CARVED INTO SKULLS AND BONES:** As a kid, I would stay busy for hours carving soap. I think we even had some special tools to carve with, but you can use a kitchen knife and a metal spoon. Carving bars of soap into fun shapes probably encouraged us to wash our hands more than once a week—and hopefully it will encourage your guests to wash up, too.

- **THE BLOODY TOWEL:** Instead of supplying your guests with a clean white towel, stain one with dark red fabric paint. Make a big, bloody handprint or even a spooky impression of a face like the shroud of Turin.

- **TOILET SEAT PRANKS:** Few household fixtures invoke as much fear and anxiety as a toilet seat does. That's why I like to mess with them. Recently I found some hot melt glue sticks that are blood colored. This allowed me to create fake blood spatter on the toilet seat that was cleanable but could not be easily removed by guests. Sure, it's rude; I'll admit it.

- **NO-TEAR TOILET PAPER:** It's a classic gag: toilet paper that won't come off the roll. Be sure to stash a few spare rolls of the real stuff under the vanity or your friends may burn you at the stake.

- **BATHTUB FULL OF BLOOD:** If you have a bathtub, why not fill it with red drink mix and float some fake human organs in there? Actually, why not fill it full of drink mix and real animal organs?

- **SILHOUETTE IN THE SHOWER:** Reenact *Psycho* from the opposite side of the shower curtain by cutting out a small silhouette of a man and placing it close to a lightbulb inside the shower. It's kind of corny, but your guests will get a kick out of it.

- **SCARY FACE IN THE WINDOW:** Does your bathroom have a window? If so, here's a fun gag. Have a headshot of one of your scruffier-looking guy friends enlarged to life size, then tape it on the outside of the window looking in. This fake peeping Tom is sure to get a reaction.

- **FAKE MICE:** Taking away much of the light in your bathroom is a fun idea because it will allow you to plant fake mice in the corner and scare people with them. Obscure reality just a bit and it'll be a cinch to freak out the musophobes.

- **A WORD ABOUT BLACK LIGHTS:** Black lights make everything look cool and spooky. Unfortunately, they aren't great for your bathroom. You see, black light illuminates urine quite well, and I think we will all be much better off not knowing the location of any urine splatter.

Living Head on a Platter

WHEN IT COMES TO CAKE DECORATING AND DECOUPAGE, you may not want to challenge the goody-goodies to a smackdown. If they are truly goody-goodies, they've been doing these things since the days when you ate canned soup direct from the can. But if you want to take on the fine art of the centerpiece, they'll never see it coming. "Why would someone so cool work on something as useless and outdated as a centerpiece?" they'll wonder. Of course, we all know the answer. We are going to make cool centerpieces to piss them off. One of my favorites is the head-on-a-table illusion. It is an old sideshow trick that uses two mirrors to fool people into thinking they can see under the table. I know this trick seems a little bit too easy, but magicians worldwide have used it to fool audiences again and again. You can use it to fool and delight your guests.

YOU'LL NEED:

- **Any old table with four legs** (you'll be cutting a hole in it, so avoid valuable antiques)

- **2 mirrors as tall and wide as the table** (you'll be gluing them to the table legs)

- **A handsaw or jigsaw**

- **A tablecloth** (it should hang just over the edge of the table)

- **Some lettuce leaves** (or other tempting garnish to surround your head)

- **A glue gun** (to attach the mirrors to the table legs)

- **A dark corner in your dining room or hallway** (the illusion works better if it's obscured by shadows)

Be the Centerpiece of Attention

Star in Your Own Sideshow

1. **SAW** a hole in the center of the table. The hole should be large enough to **STICK** your head through.

2. **GLUE** the tablecloth to the table. Once it is glued, **CUT** a slit in it to poke your head through.

3. **GLUE** the two mirrors to the backside of the table legs. They should form a *V* shape that you will **HIDE** behind. **POINT** the tip of the *V* at your audience, so they will only see the reflection of the dining room walls in the mirror. They will **BELIEVE** they are seeing **UNDERNEATH** the table to the other side of the room.

4. **TEST** out the illusion on a friend. You may need to move things away from the walls first so there are no inconsistencies between the **REFLECTION** in the mirror and the opposite wall. If your party guests see a potted plant in the mirror but not on the opposite wall, the jig is up.

5. When you are ready to go live, **POKE** your head through the hole and ask an assistant to arrange the lettuce leaves or some other **GARNISH** around your neck. How's that for a **UNIQUE CENTERPIECE**?

More Kickass Centerpieces

Here are some other centerpiece ideas to horrify the goody-goodies.

TABLE THEME	RELATED CENTERPIECE
A street with yellow lines and tire tracks	Road kill
Mad scientist's laboratory	Specimen jar
Crime scene investigation	A severed head, if you happen to have one on hand
Slaughterhouse	A roasted cow's heart (visit your local butcher)
Autopsy in progress	Brain Goo (for recipe, see page 92)
Jungle party	Shrunken heads (make some by dehydrating apples and carving faces on them)
Luau	Angry tiki pumpkin god (for carving ideas, see page 47)

Kiddie Entertainment

Ever since child labor was made illegal, the parents of the world have had to entertain their children. This can become a problem when you want to have fun yourself. In order to keep the good times rolling (and the kids off my back), I try to trick them into helping me at every turn. Here are some thoughts on how you can keep the young'ins meaningfully engaged at a pumpkin-carving party.

- **SCOOPING PUMPKIN GUTS:** Kids love digging into the pumpkin and pulling out all of the seeds. Sure, they'll get frustrated after a short time, but I have a cure for that as well. Make sure you have about 10 different things to use to scoop the pumpkin guts. That way, they can try different techniques. By the time they have experimented with the ice cream scoop, the gravy ladle, the pumpkin gooper, and the putty knife most of the dirty work will be done.

- **SEPARATING THE PUMPKINSEEDS FROM THE PULP:** Everyone likes to roast and eat pumpkinseeds, but not many people like the work of separating the seeds from the pumpkin flesh. Fortunately, kids love this type of disgusting, tactile task. Give them a few buckets to work with and let them have at it.

- **WASHING THE PUMPKINS:** It's October now and the summer months are long gone, but kids will relish one last opportunity to use the garden hose. Why not invite them to wash the dirt off the pumpkins to get them ready for carving? Give them a big scrub brush and let them do their thing. They can also fill a big washtub full of water and dunk the finished pumpkins in it to get rid of the pulpy mess that carving leaves behind.

- **CARVING THE PUMPKINS:** My friends seem to be a fairly lazy bunch, but their tween-age kids are workaholics. Whenever I host a pumpkin-carving party it is these kids that do all of the prep work. Their parents just sit around and drink beer. God bless them both.

- **WAITERS AND WAITRESSES:** Kids love to do adult things and serving food falls into that category. I like to capitalize on their enthusiasm by giving them appetizers to hand out, or by asking them to take orders for the grill. Just make sure they aren't taking drink orders—unless the drink is rootbeer!

Demented Ways to Dress Up Your Baby

As a parent of three, I try really hard to give my kids every opportunity in life. They get the finest care and see the best doctors. Their college funds are stuffed with book royalties. But come Halloween, somehow I can't resist dressing them up in costumes most good parents would call unsuitable. Here are some outtakes; you be the judge.

- **A MOP:** Babies make enough of a mess. Why not turn their crawling into some useful work? Take their pajamas and glue some new dust mops on them. Pretty soon you'll have the cleanest hardwood floors in town. Watch out for sneezing fits or stuff they shouldn't put in their mouths (babies can get clogged up just like your Dyson or Dirt Devil).

- **A MEMBER OF KISS:** Whether it is Gene (the Demon), Ace (the Spaceman), Peter (the Catman), or even Paul (the Star Child), no Kiss character makes an acceptable costume for your baby. Sure, Kiss rocked out, but they didn't rock hard enough that you should dress your kid in honor of them.

- **THE CLOACA:** Not many people will get the reference to Belgian artist Wim Delvoye's poop-making modern art piece, but everyone knows what comes out of kids. Simply labeling the costume "food in" and "poop out" should suffice.

- **A PACK OF SMOKES OR A BOTTLE OF BOOZE:** I hate smoking as much as anyone, but I still think there is some perverted humor in dressing your kid up like a pack of smokes. Imagine the looks of disgust you will get as you cruise an upscale neighborhood with your Camel-costumed kid. While I do enjoy drinking, I think that dressing your kid up as a bottle of booze is not offensive enough to be funny. So, if you are going for vice-related laughs, go for the pack of smokes.

Bloody Brain Shots

ANYONE CAN SERVE BEER AND SPARKLING WINE. At your next Halloween bash, how about presenting this unusual shot? It looks like a bloody brain and has the mouthfeel of curdled milk, but tastes something like Juicy Fruit gum. The trick is in the slow application of the grenadine syrup. This recipe makes one shot.

YOU'LL NEED:

- **1 ounce peach schnapps** (you should have some in the back of your cabinet)
- **1 teaspoon Bailey's Irish Cream** (that's your brains)
- **Grenadine** (and there's the blood)
- **Shot glass** (clear glass is essential for maximum impact)

Let the Evil Begin

1. **POUR** the peach schnapps into a shot glass.

2. **FLOAT** the Bailey's Irish Cream on top of the schnapps.

3. **DRIBBLE** a few drops of grenadine on top of the Bailey's. There's no hurry: Take it nice and **SLOW**.

4. **SERVE**. Hope that your first victim does not **RETCH**.

5. Repeat steps 1 through 4 on your next **UNSUSPECTING VICTIM**, until everyone at the party has had some bloody brains. (You are the bartender so you are officially **EXEMPT** from having to down these repulsive shots.)

I Don't Know How Zombies Get Drunk, But This Might Be It

Scary Drinks

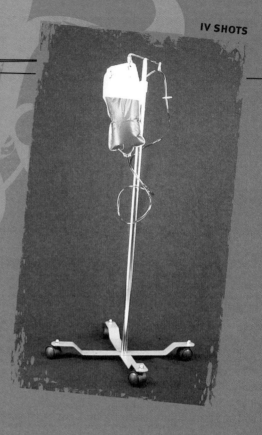

Looking for some creative cocktails to serve at your Halloween party? Of course you are! Here are some other fun libations sure to keep your guests entertained.

IV SHOTS

Phlebotomy meets mixology in this unusual presentation. You'll see: An IV bag is the perfect dispenser for booze.

1. Procure an IV bag and WRITE something witty on it. I wrote: "Blood Type: O, Patient: C. Dracula."

2. RINSE the bag thoroughly. LOCK the clamp on the bag so that it won't spill when you fill it.

3. MIX 2 cans (12 ounces each) cranberry juice concentrate, 2 cans (12 ounces each) grape juice concentrate, and one 750 ml bottle vodka in a pitcher.

4. FILL the IV bag with the booze. HANG it on an IV stand (visit your friendly neighborhood medical supply company) or a simple hook.

5. INVITE your guests to step up for a TRANSFUSION in a shot glass.

Oh yeah, one other thing: IV bags come sealed so if you can't open them, you'll have to use an enema bag. That's right, an enema bag. Use a new one, dude, not one you borrowed from your aunt Mildred. P.S. Don't tell any of my friends that they have been drinking out of enema bags for the last few October 31s.

EYEBALL MARTINIS

A martini is a drink of sophistication, but I am notoriously unsophisticated, so I like to create martinis that don't want to be consumed, then drink them anyway. It's like crossing the libations' union picket line. Here's how you can cross that line, too:

1. COMBINE 2 ounces gin with a splash of vermouth in a cocktail shaker.

2. ADD some crushed ice to the shaker. Shake and then let it sit for a moment.

3. Use a toothpick to ATTACH two cocktail olives to one another. Try to make them look like cute little staring eyes.

4. PLACE the olive eyes in a martini glass and POUR the shaken martini over them.

5. With a small piece of tape and another toothpick, CONSTRUCT a little flag. Stick the flag into the eyes so that it rises above the drink's surface. Make a few different flags so that the martinis can protest their own consumption in a variety of ways, from "Martinis Are Murder" and "Gin Is Sin" to "No Vermouth In Your Mouth" and "Drink More Beer."

TOM'S PUMPKIN PUNCH

Serving a spicy fall punch in a hollowed-out pumpkin is a great idea. You'll be happy to know that the pumpkin probably won't leak. Probably. If that isn't enough reassurance for you, don't be afraid to use a craft pumpkin in place of a real one or you could line the pumpkin with a large plastic bag. If you do use a real pumpkin for a punchbowl, be sure to clean it out pretty well. When guests stir the punch, they won't want to stir up pumpkin guts and seeds.

1. Using your gutted pumpkin as a punchbowl, COMBINE 1 part apple cider, 2 parts ginger ale, and 1 part spiced rum, stirring until well mixed. You can leave out the rum for a great kids' punch.

2. If you want something cool to float in the punch, MOLD some frozen lemonade into the shape of a brain. (See Brain Goo, page 92.)

URINE SAMPLE GELATIN SHOTS

Getting old sucks. There was a time when gelatin shots were really cool. I enjoyed that time and guzzled my share of them. Unfortunately, that was a few administrations ago. Now, gelatin shots are no longer cool. This is because your mom will do gelatin shots, and anything that your mom will do is, by definition, not cool. I'm hoping that I can bring back the gelatin shot by making them a bit edgier with the addition of a little bitty sign.

1. Following the package directions, MAKE one 3-ounce package of lemon gelatin, but when it comes time to add the cold water, SUBSTITUTE vodka.

2. Serve the gelatin shots in specimen cups. ADD a small sign that says "Urine Samples."

Pumpkin Vomiting Guacamole

HERE'S AN APPETIZER SO GROSS only the very brave (or very hungry) will eat it. I'm sure you could just look at the picture and figure out how to make it, but since you insist, I've provided a puking pumpkin tutorial below.

YOU'LL NEED:

- **1 small pumpkin** (about the size of a baby's head)
- **CARVING TOOLS: pumpkin-carving saw** (a jigsaw might be overkill), **big metal spoon** (to scoop out the guts), **angle grinder** (to flay the eyebrows), **paring knife** (to carve the jalapeños)
- **1½ cups guacamole** (I just bought the kind sold in a tub, but you can make your own if you are like that)
- **3 or 4 fresh jalapeño chile peppers** (if they are very hot, that will dissuade nibblers, too)
- **Plenty of tortilla chips** (your starving guests are sure to gorge on these)
- **Serving platter**

Reuse. Recycle.

Must I Spell It Out?

1. Using the pumpkin-carving saw, **CUT OUT** the bottom of the pumpkin and **SCOOP OUT** all of the guts and seeds with a big metal spoon. Do a **THOROUGH JOB**.

2. Using the saw, **CARVE** a puking face on your pumpkin. If you can't remember what that looks like, look at the picture that is within 7 inches of the words you are reading right now.

3. **WASH** and **DRY** the pumpkin so that it is clean. Put it on the platter. Using the paring knife, **CARVE** silly faces on the jalapeños.

4. Right before guests arrive, **SPOON** some of the guacamole inside the pumpkin's mouth and the rest right in front of it. **TOP** the guacamole with the little jalapeño faces and **ARRANGE** chips around the dip.

5. You have completed your guacamole-regurgitating pumpkin. Yay, you! In a couple of hours, that guacamole is going to **TURN BROWN**, further enhancing the **REALISM** of your display.

Roasted Squash Skulls

IF YOU ARE EXPECTING a recipe for squash that makes it taste great, perhaps something like bacon but with the mouthfeel of ice cream, you have bought the wrong book. I'm not a chef and, even if I was, I doubt I could make squash appeal to people (especially children) who hate it. What I can do is make serving and eating squash entertaining. Why not turn a bunch of roasted squash (and maybe some sinister root vegetables) into a dining room massacre? Present a plate of squash skulls and invite your guests to dig in. The list of 10 Deadliest Kitchen Tools (on page 79) gives you lots of grotesque ideas for serving implements.

YOU'LL NEED:

- **CARVING TOOLS:** (an unusually clean) **carving saw, big chef's knife**, and **vegetable peeler** (Y-shaped is best)

- **Large roasting pan**

- **Large platter** (lazy folk can serve the skulls in the roasting pan)

- **Pastry brush**

- **A selection of sadistic serving utensils** (got a cleaver? perfect!)

- **8 to 10 head-shaped vegetables** (pumpkins, squash, sweet potatoes, and onions are all fair game)

- **1/2 cup (1 stick) unsalted butter**, melted

- **Salt and pepper** to taste

Surrogate Enemies

1. Think of everyone you currently **DESPISE**. Go to the grocery store and **BUY** one squash or other representative veggie for each person. Some folks will run out of enemies at eight squashes or so. Other folks may have trouble finding eight people they loathe. (Then again, those folks don't usually buy my books.)

2. **PREHEAT** the oven to 375 degrees F. Then, before you start carving, **ARRANGE** the squashes on your serving platter. That way, you can map out an especially **TORTUROUS TABLEAU**.

3. Using the big chef's knife and vegetable peeler, **CARVE FACES** on your squashes and other veggies. Give them sullen, depressed expressions. Don't make them look angry; that will make eating

them too easy. You want them to look like **VICTIMS LINED UP ON THE BUFFET** so your guests will be forced out of their comfort zone. **TIP:** The faces will sink a little as the squashes roast, so carve them a little higher up than you normally would.

4. **ARRANGE** the whole squashes in the roasting pan. **BRUSH** them with half of the melted butter, and **SEASON** with salt and pepper to taste.

5. **ROAST** small squashes and veggies for 1 hour, medium for 1 hour 15 minutes, and large for 1 hour 30 minutes. Halfway through roasting, baste with the rest of the melted butter. You know the skulls are done when a **SKEWER** goes through them easily.

6. Let the roasted skulls cool for about 15 minutes, then **TRANSFER** them to the serving platter. You can **STAB** one serving utensil into each skull, or you can put all the utensils in the skull of a single **MURDER VICTIM** as the other squashes look on in horror.

The Feeling Is Mutual: You Don't Like Squash and They Don't Like Being Eaten

The 10 Deadliest Kitchen Utensils

The utensil drawer is probably the most lethal place in the house. I'm sure all of these items could kill you in a matter of minutes. Of course, the only thing I suggest you slay with them is a pumpkin or head of lettuce. Chopped salad, anyone?

1. **CLEAVER:** I own one, but it scares the crap out of me. I bought it after watching too many episodes of *Yan Can Cook*. I would rather handle a chainsaw than that evil thing. It is heavy, out of balance, and doesn't seem like it would stop cutting when it hits bone. Youch!

2. **GIGANTIC CARVING KNIFE:** Ever see one of those 20-inch-long carving knives? Who needs that thing? Is it used to butcher entire sides of beef, or do some people like to slice their watermelons the long way?

3. **CHEESE GRATER:** They should just cut with the bullcrap and call this thing a "knuckle bleeder."

4. **MANDOLINE/V-SLICER:** Cooking shows often recommend these, but in my opinion, they're way too sharp to be worth the risk. Every time I effortlessly pass a potato over a mandoline, I think, "This thing could take off half my arm."

5. **CORKSCREW:** I use a corkscrew without trepidation, but if you think I am going to put that thing within 1 foot of my eyeball, you are oh-so-wrong.

6. **METAL MEAT TENDERIZER:** Need I say more? If you own one of these and it's not still in the packaging, I'm nervous.

7. **METAL SKEWERS:** Maybe my imagination is too wild, but I can think of at least 10 ways these things could kill me.

8. **BLENDER/FOOD PROCESSOR:** If it can crush ice cubes with ease, imagine what it would do to the slender bones in your finger. I can imagine it well enough that I have already come up with an alternate way to push the buttons on my cell phone. (Note: It doesn't involve a trained monkey.)

9. **MARINADE INJECTOR:** This thing is like a giant hypodermic needle. The tip is too dull, the needle too large, and it dispenses by the ounce. In other words, this tool is the stuff of nightmares.

10. **ROLLING PIN AND CAST-IRON FRYING PAN:** These don't seem that deadly, but if comic strips have taught me anything, it is that when you come home late from the bar, your wife is sure to attack you with one of these jobs. Watch your back.

Meat Head

SURE, DELI MEAT IS DELICIOUS, but have you ever really thought about what's in it? Those white bits in the salami? That's fat. The recipe for bologna? Grind the poorest-quality pork scraps with some chemical preservatives. But don't let me ruin your next picnic. Instead, here is a way to emphasize just how gross deli meats really are. I didn't invent the Meat Head, but I can say that I thoroughly enjoyed making this one for my guests. Some folks even dared to eat it.

YOU'LL NEED:

- **2 pearl onions** (these will be the eyes, of course)

- **Plastic skull** (found at your local craft or party supply store; a rough-textured one will help the deli meat stick)

- **1 pound salami** (the kind with peppercorns in it would look extra gross)

- **1 pound deli ham** (the cheap stuff looks gnarlier)

- **1 pound assorted cheese slices** (don't break the bank; Kraft singles will do)

- **2 baguettes** (to create a skull and crossbones theme)

- **Sandwich fixins** (mayo, mustard, pickles)

- **Large platter** (if you don't have one, a clean cutting board would work, too)

Eyeball, Anyone?

1. **PEEL** the pearl onions until they look white. Don't cut off the root ends; these will be the **PUPILS**. Using your knife, **CARVE** the onions so they will fit snugly in the eye sockets of your skull. After you **CRAM** both onions into the skull, point the eyeballs so that they are both looking in the same direction (or not, if you want to make a **CROSS-EYED** Meat Head).

You Gotta Have Ham

2. Getting the meat to **STICK** to the skull is a bit tricky. You can't use glue or rubber cement because that would harm your guests, so you have to be **CRAFTY**. Fortunately, I realized I could harness the same **FORCES OF NATURE** that attach a man's comb-over to his skull. Here's how the **COMB-OVER TECHNIQUE** works:

a. First, **SLICE** about half of the salami pieces in half. **SLAP** a half moon of salami on the skull, so the straight edge runs vertically. Hold it there as you slap another piece of salami on top, so it **OVERLAPS** one-third of the first piece of salami. **REPEAT** with additional half slices until you reach the crown of the head.

b. When you can barely keep the salami pieces stuck to the skull, **CAP** them off with a whole piece of salami on the crown of the head. This piece, which sort of resembles a skullcap, will help hold all of those other pieces on. Or, to continue the comb-over analogy, the pieces on the far side **FORCE** the other pieces against the skull. It is a strange balance, but I guess all of the fat and preservatives work together. No glue (or toupee) required.

c. **REPEAT** steps a and b until the sides, back, and top of the skull are **COMPLETELY COVERED** in salami.

3 Adding salami flesh to the face is **TRICKIER** because the face has more contours. **SLICE** three or four pieces of the salami into strips and rely on the **NATURAL CLING** of the meat to make it **STICK** to the face.

4 When you're finished with the salami, **SLICE** the ham into strips. If you use cheap deli ham, it will **STICK** fairly well to the salami and the entire head will have a **SINEWY** sort of look that is hard to beat.

It's Party Time

5 **COVER** your lunch meat sculpture with aluminum foil (never cling wrap) and **REFRIGERATE** it. When it's time to serve, carefully place your Meat Head on a **BIG PLATTER**, surrounded by cheese slices, baguettes, and all the sandwich fixins. Invite your guests to **DIG IN**.

Hamming It Up Has Never Been So Disgusting

Roasted Human Being

I'M SURPRISED that I didn't think of this sooner. I mean, I have liked cooking since high school and I have hated my fellow man since then as well. Why had I not combined the two things before? If you also like to cook and hate people, you'll enjoy serving this dish at a Halloween party, too. You are sure to be the talk of the town.

You may be surprised to hear that this is actually a tasty and fairly easy-to-make Halloween feast. Perhaps it will begin to rival the traditional turkey dinner as the most popular feast of the year. It is made from some favorite party foods and will easily feed a crowd of 40 to 60. If you have fewer guests to feed, consider serving a smaller, less involved corpse. You may decide to replace some of the limbs with loaves of bread or vegetables, or omit the pig's feet and oxtails or other things no one will eat.

YOU'LL NEED:

FOR THE UPPER BODY SKELETON

- **2 full racks of pork ribs** (they should be symmetrical, not from the same side of the hog)

- **Some rib rub** (that's seasoning for you non-grilling types)

- **A dozen oxtails** (these make a convincing spine)

- **4 country-style pork ribs or beef ribs** (for the clavicles and upper arms)

- **2 ham hocks** (for the shoulders)

FOR THE GUTS

- **4 pounds assorted sausages** (throw in some turkey sausages for the no-red-meat crowd)

- **Vegetables:** onions, squash, broccoli, cauliflower (anything you like!)

FOR THE SKULL

- **1 pear-shaped pumpkin** (a little larger than a human head)

- **CARVING TOOLS: jigsaw** (or pumpkin-carving saw), **big metal spoon**

FOR THE FOREARMS AND HANDS

- **2 turkey drumsticks** (for the forearms)
- **2 pork chops** (for the hands, of course)
- **10 breakfast sausages** (for extra-tasty fingers)

FOR THE LUNGS

- **1 box instant mashed potatoes** (13.3 ounces)
- **3¹/₃ cups milk**
- **1 stick butter** (¹/₂ cup)
- **Salt and pepper** to taste

FOR THE PELVIS, LEGS, AND FEET

- **1 pork shoulder** (sometimes called a pork butt or Boston butt)
- **2 whole legs of lamb** (extravagant? sure it is!)
- **1 rib roast or prime rib roast** (choose one large enough to contain two bones)
- **2 pig's feet**

FOR THE BLOOD

- **1 big bottle of your favorite barbecue sauce** (18 ounces)

OTHER EQUIPMENT

- **Plastic tablecloth** (to protect your table)
- **A very big grill** (I had to use two: mine and my friend Matt's)
- **A meat thermometer** (helps you cook the body parts just right)

The Meat on His Bones

1. My friend, it is time to prep the flesh and bones. The ribcage is first. Take each rack of ribs and **TRIM** them so they look like human ribs. (I **REMOVED** the five smallest bones and trimmed all of the meat from the ends.) Then **EVENLY COAT** all of the pork parts (the country-ribs, hocks, feet, and pork shoulder) with a dry rub.

2. Grab the legs of lamb and **REPEATEDLY STAB THEM WITH A KNIFE**. Fill each gash with a half clove of garlic. Then **RUB SALT INTO THE WOUNDS** and all over the flesh of those same legs.

3. **APPLY** liberal amounts of salt and pepper to all of the beef (ribs, oxtails, and especially the prime rib) and the turkey legs. The vegetables may be an afterthought but you should still find time to **DROWN THEM** in a bath of olive oil seasoned with salt and pepper.

4. Barbecuing is one of the **GREAT AMERICAN PASTIMES**, so I won't try to tell you the best way to do it, because you probably already know. **FIRE UP YOUR GRILL** and use your

favorite method to **BARBECUE** all of this meat until it tastes irresistible.

5. I do have some **TIPS ON TIMING** though. The pork butt, pig's feet, and ham hocks will take the longest to cook (usually 3 to 4 hours), followed by the ribs and legs of lamb (typically 2 to 3 hours). Next come the roasted vegetables and prime rib (90 to 120 minutes), and finally the quick-cooking sausages, pork chops, and grilled vegetables. Time it right and everything will be **SUCCULENT AND JUICY** at the same time. Time it wrong and you could be the next corpse eaten at the cannibal feast. A meat thermometer is your **GO-TO TOOL** here.

Carve the Skull

6. Nothing complements a fall barbecue like pumpkins, so while the meat is on the grill, **CARVE** and gut a pumpkin skull. **TURN** the pear-shaped pumpkin upside down. Use a carving knife and big metal spoon to **GUT** it from the bottom (which is now the top of the skull), then **CARVE** away. Cut out eye sockets, nostrils, and a mouth.

Other Nasty Bits

7. Making the lungs is easy, too. **FOLLOW THE DIRECTIONS** on a box of instant mashed potatoes. Before making this corpse, I had never made **INSTANT MASHED POTATOES**—I always stuck my nose in the air and made the real kind. You know what? They taste just about

the same and they are a million times easier. After making the potatoes, let them **COOL** for about 30 minutes so they aren't too hot to handle.

8. If you want **MORE BLOOD**, you can use barbecue sauce. The dark reddish-brown color looks fairly bloodlike without a fuss, and it **TASTES GREAT**. **WARM** it up in the microwave, if you like.

Lay Out the Victim

9. You'll need a big table to display your corpse. I used a 4x8-foot sheet of plywood on sawhorses. To **PREVENT SPLINTERS**, I laid out some plastic tablecloths. Cookout prep and **CLEANUP** doesn't get much easier than that.

10 START from the head and **WORK DOWNWARD**. You may need to **CHOP** a hunk off the back of the pumpkin skull to make it sit right.

11 Next, **SITUATE** the spine by arranging your oxtails. Add the collarbones and shoulder blades (country-style ribs and ham hocks).

12 **PLOP** down all of the mashed potatoes and **SHAPE** them into two big lungs. If you'd like your corpse to show some smoker's damage, **TAINT** the lungs with black food coloring (equal proportions of red, blue, and yellow food coloring should do the trick). **REST** the barbecued ribs on top to give the impression of a full chest cavity.

13 **FORM** the guts from the vegetables and sausages. I wish I could have used **ONE CONTINUOUS LENGTH** of sausage, but I wasn't able to find turkey sausage of that type.

14 **SET** the arms and hands in place by positioning the beef ribs for biceps, the turkey legs for forearms, and the pork chops and breakfast sausages for the hands and fingers. To make the thumbs shorter than the fingers, **SNAP OFF A CHUNK** of sausage and eat it.

15 A pork shoulder doesn't seem like it would make a good pelvis, but I was surprised at how convincing (not to mention tasty) it looked. Perhaps I was born to re-create **DEATH AND DISMEMBERMENT**?

16 Legs? Nothing I have ever experienced looked as simultaneously delicious and disgusting as those legs of lamb. Especially cool was how the bones were **JUTTING OUT** of the corpse's knees. To form the calves, **SLICE** the prime rib in half.

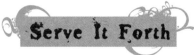

Serve It Forth

17 For an optional finishing touch, you can **POUR** and **BRUSH** barbecue sauce or gravy all over your roasted human. This creates **RANDOM SPLATTER** and especially **SAUCY BITS**.

18 Invite everyone to **DIG IN**. Be sure to **PROVIDE** plenty of napkins and have a couple of carving knives handy. When I came up with this concept, I thought no one would want to eat my roasted human corpse, but it turned out to be one of the easiest, most successful party dinners I have ever thrown. Either my friends and I are **BARBARIANS**, or this really is a fun party gambit.

Tastes Like Chicken

Vegetarians Can Be Cannibals, Too

Every Adam needs an Eve so I began to think that my corpse needed a bride. Of course, she would have to be different in some significant way, so I figured she could be made of vegetables. Here are some tips on how to construct a 100-percent vegetarian corpse; serve it raw, roasted, steamed, or sautéed.

- SKULL: Spaghetti squash (use the fibers for hair)
- COLLARBONES: Celery
- VERTEBRAE: Sliced mushrooms
- ARMS: Cucumbers and carrots
- HANDS AND FINGERS: Green peppers and green beans
- LUNGS: Dip
- RIBS: Asparagus with tomato breasts (for a female corpse)
- GUTS: A salad or heaps of coleslaw
- PELVIS: One-half cauliflower head
- LEGS: Zucchini and summer squash
- FEET: Banana peppers

Wow! I feel like I'm on fire with this line of thinking. Next, I'll make a kid out of desserts, then a dog out of bread, then a cat out of cheese, and a pet fish out of fish. I can make a parakeet out of pickles and a squirrel out of chicken, and a chicken out of squirrel. A pet goat out of lamb and a bunny out of chocolate are within the realm of possibility, too. Whew! The possibilities make the mind (and stomach) reel.

Banana Pudding Blob

AS DESSERT TREATS GO, banana pudding is one of the all-time greats. Every time I make the stuff, everyone gobbles it up. So, I have had to resort to scare tactics in order to enjoy my favorite party dessert. First, I make a large display out of the banana pudding. This way, anyone who hates attention will avoid eating it. Next, I put some toy animals and people in the banana pudding to dissuade the vegetarians. Finally, I color the banana pudding in strange colors. Kids hate food that is the wrong color. The only remaining folks are those brave enough to grab the grub no matter who is watching. That's us.

YOU'LL NEED:

- **An electric mixer** (I'm sorry if you don't own one; borrow one)

- **A giant mixing bowl** (we are making a lot of pudding here)

FOR THE PUDDING

- **2 boxes vanilla wafers** (12 ounces per box)

- **4 packages instant vanilla pudding** (5.9-ounces each)

- **¹/₂ gallon whole milk** (or 2 percent if you want to pretend to make this dessert low-fat)

- **1 can sweetened condensed milk** (14 ounces)

- **8 ripe bananas**

FOR THE WHIPPED CREAM

- **One 16-ounce container whipping cream**

- **¹/₂ teaspoon vanilla extract**

- **¹/₂ cup granulated sugar**

- **Liquid food coloring** (all colors welcome)

FOR THE MOVIE SCENERY

- **A disposable tablecloth**

- **Aluminum foil** (to create a street)

- **Graham crackers** (these will be the sidewalk)

- **Miniature buildings, cars, and people** (I used HO scale buildings and people from a train set and Matchbox model cars)

World's Most Extreme Banana Pudding

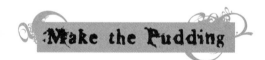

Make the Pudding

1. **SMASH** the vanilla wafers into a few pieces each. Don't crumble them, just **BREAK** them up a bit. While I prefer the flavor and texture of whole wafers, the Blob won't look convincing if it is made out of a bunch of disks. Put the wafers in a big bowl.

2. **SLICE** half of the bananas and then **MASH** the rest. Make the pieces look random but keep them bite-size. **ADD** these to the bowl with the wafers.

3. **MIX** the pudding mix, milk, and condensed milk with an electric mixer. Sure, you could do this by hand, but why bother? You'll also be using the mixer to make whipped cream soon.

4. **POUR** the pudding over the wafers and **STIR** the whole mess up. Cover the bowl with plastic wrap to prevent it from forming a gross skin. Put the pudding-wafer mix in the fridge. **WASH** the mixer bowl and put it in the fridge, too. Making whipped cream is easier if the mixer bowl is cold.

5. **CHILL** out for an hour or so while the pudding chills.

Whip It Up

6. Get the mixer ready. **POUR** the cream, sugar, and vanilla into the chilled bowl and **JUST BEAT IT**. "Showin' how funky strong is your fight." **SING** the song while you whip the cream. Don't walk away. **STOP** beating as soon as the whipped cream is whipped cream. Go too far and you'll make butter. Just beat it.

7. **DIVIDE** the whipped cream between three different bowls. **USE** some food coloring to make one bowl of whipped cream red (this takes quite a bit of red food coloring) and one greenish blue (use a few drops of both green and blue food coloring); **LEAVE** the last bowl of whipped cream white.

8. If I asked you to **"FOLD"** the whipped cream into the pudding, would you know what I was talking about? No? OK, **PUT** the red whipped

cream on top of the pudding; **MIX** it only nine times. **PUT** the greenish-blue whipped cream on top of that; **MIX** it only nine times. **PUT** the white whipped cream on top of that; **MIX** it only nine times. Why didn't you mix it more? Because it will **GO FLAT** if you mix it too much. Also, blobs are made up of a **BUNCH OF COLORS**, not just a single color.

9 **COVER** the blob pudding mixture with plastic wrap and **REFRIGERATE** it for up to 24 hours. Some folks say it **TASTES BETTER** that way.

Set the Scene

10 Before your party, **SET UP** the town for your Blob to destroy. **LAY OUT** a disposable tablecloth to protect your dining table. **MAKE** a street out of aluminum foil and graham cracker sidewalks. **ADD** the miniature buildings, leaving plenty of room for the Blob.

11 Just before your guests arrive, **PUT** the Blob in place. **POSITION** the figurines last. **MAKE A SCENE** (with the figures, not your guests). I used army men and innocent citizens to create a town under attack. A drop of red food coloring on the figures inside the Blob makes them look bloody. Only **HUNGRY GUESTS** can save them!

The Blob Fun Facts

If you plan to make a dessert that represents a scene from a movie, it helps to know something about the movie. So, here is your refresher course on *The Blob*:

- The 1958 movie *The Blob* was one of the first horror films shot in color, and for its day, it had a fairly large budget. The result was a drive-in movie success.

- It was also the screen debut of Steve McQueen, who played the lead character. McQueen's later film career (including *The Great Escape*, *The Thomas Crown Affair*, and *The Magnificent Seven*) helped ensure that *The Blob* stayed in the public consciousness.

- The Blob hatches from inside a meteor that lands on Earth. As it engulfs more and more people, the Blob gets bigger and bigger.

- At one point, the Blob attacks the local movie theater. This probably terrified theatergoers, as at the time, this plotline was a new cinematic trick.

- The army finally drops the Blob into the Arctic. The Blob is vanquished. Or is it?

Brain Goo

A FEW YEARS AGO I bought a gelatin mold that's shaped (more or less) like a human brain. Although I personally don't care much for gelatin (I prefer its equally amorphous but chocolate-flavored cousin, pudding), I sure do like making things that look like brains. For this book, I decided just molding a brain and putting it on a platter wasn't enough. So, I added some cool finishing touches, like eyeballs, a pool of blood, and a bit of spinal cord to complete the picture. Here's how you, too, can keep your party guests from eating all of your food.

YOU'LL NEED:

FOR THE BRAIN

- **1 brain-shaped gelatin mold** (I bought my 18-ounce mold at a Halloween store)
- **Nonstick cooking spray**
- **5 small boxes lemon gelatin** (3 ounces each)
- **1 small box grape gelatin** (3 ounces)
- **One 16-ounce can evaporated skim milk** (make sure you go with fat-free)
- **2 big bowls and a whisk**
- **1 kitchen towel**

FOR THE BLOOD

- **1 large box strawberry gelatin** (6 ounces)

FOR THE EYEBALLS AND SPINAL CORD

- **2 crispy rice cereal treats** (my publisher said not to use the brand name, but you know what I'm talking about)
- **1 cherry** (the maraschino ones are nice and moist)
- **Licorice rope** (preferably both black and red)

I Tried to Donate My Brain, But They Said I Had to Die First

3. **MAKE THE GELATIN** in your brain mold according to package directions, except **SUBSTITUTE** the evaporated skim milk for an equal proportion of cold water.

4. **ARRANGE** the kitchen towel in a **DOUGHNUT SHAPE** in one of the big bowls. Place the gelatin-filled mold inside the towel doughnut. The towel will keep the mold horizontal while the gelatin chills. Transfer the bowl to the refrigerator until **FULLY SET**, at least 5 hours.

Gruesome Garnish

5. While the brain **CHILLS OUT**, let's prepare the pool of blood with the eyeballs and spinal cord floating in it. To make the blood, **FOLLOW THE DIRECTIONS** on the package of strawberry gelatin. **POUR** it in your serving tray and **REFRIGERATE**. That was easy.

6. To make the eyeballs, **SQUISH** the crispy rice treats into two eyeball shapes. **CUT** the cherry in half and **PUSH** one half into each of the crispy rice eyeballs. That was easy, too.

7. **PULL** apart your licorice ropes into separate strands. Then **RANDOMLY WIND** them back together. You have just made a spinal cord that's **GOOD TO EAT**.

8. After the strawberry gelatin has set for about 1 hour, **ARRANGE** the spinal cord and eyeballs in it.

9. Just before the party, **WIGGLE** the brain mold around to loosen up the brain. **PLOP** it out into your hands and then place it **RIGHT-SIDE UP** on top of the pool of blood. **YUM!**

Bottle a Frontal Lobotomy

1. For easy removal later, **SPRAY** your brain mold with nonstick cooking spray. (I learned this lesson the hard way.)

2. If your brain mold is 18 ounces, like mine, **FOLLOW MY INGREDIENTS LIST** precisely. (The combination of 5 small lemon gelatins and 1 small grape gelatin tastes like the kind of **LEMONADE** you buy at an unsupervised five-year-old's lemonade stand, but it looks great.) If you have a bigger brain mold, you will need to **DO THE MATH** to figure out equivalent proportions for the ingredients. This should not be a problem if your brain is **BIGGER THAN MINE**.

ACKNOWLEDGMENTS

FIRST, I would like to thank my wife for being wonderful, beautiful, and cool. I would also like to thank her dad for not teaching her to avoid men like me. My kids deserve special thanks because they went to bed on time, allowing me the opportunity to write this book. Thanks to everyone I work with at PriveCo because they never blinked an eye when I brought outrageous Halloween stuff into the office, even when everyone else was celebrating Fourth of July. My friend Gabby also seemed to know how to kick-start my ideas when they got stale. Of course, I would also like to thank my mom, dad, brothers, sister, and other family members.

My people at Penguin are the best: Marian Lizzi, Tom Haushalter, and freelance editor Sarah Scheffel deserve special mention. One reason I like to write these books is that I get to have dinner with some of the greatest people in publishing once a year. My manager, Arty Miller, deserves a thank$ with a dollar sign in it. This book was designed by Stephanie Stislow of Stislow Design+Illustration, who helped make my stuff look pretty cool.

I would like to not thank my neighbor. The police have knocked on my door twice during the writing of this book, and judging from the conversations I had with them, the same person keeps calling to complain about me. To this neighbor, I say, "You are a moron and the cops are tired of following up on your paranoid visions. Stop it."

INDEX

FOR THOSE ABOUT TO CARVE...

BEFORE THERE WAS *Extreme Halloween*, there was *Extreme Pumpkins*...and then *Extreme Pumpkins II*. Master carver and patron saint of the jack-o'-lantern Tom Nardone wrote a renegade guide to crazy carving, and then thrilled fans with an over-the-top sequel that's even more strange and inspiring than the original. In these two outrageous volumes you'll find everything you need to carve the weirdest and most truly frightening pumpkin on the block (and then some).

Highlights include...

- **PUKING PUMPKIN**
- **CANNIBAL PUMPKIN**
- **MOONING PUMPKIN**

- **PROBLEM CHILD PUMPKIN**
- **CRO-MAGNON PUMPKIN**
- **SUBURBAN-NIGHTMARE PUMPKIN**

ABOUT THE AUTHOR

TOM NARDONE is the founder of ExtremePumpkins.com, an alternative pumpkin-carving website with a large and twisted following. His first book, *Extreme Pumpkins*, was a national bestseller that led to a pumpkin-guts-filled appearance on *Live with Regis & Kelly*. His second book, *Extreme Pumpkins II*, was another national bestseller that landed him (and his pumpkin-thumping tool) on *Late Night with Conan O' Brien*. He lives in Detroit with three kids and an extremely tolerant wife.